Electronic Engineering Series

Editor: Professor W. A. Gambling
  D Sc, CEng, FIEE, FIERE
  University of Southampton

Electronic Power Supplies

Electronic Engineering Series

This series of monographs provides a coverage of fundamental topics in the early years of undergraduate study, supplemented with more advanced topics of a specialist nature.

Titles for early publication

Electronic Power Supplies, G. N. Patchett (*University of Bradford*)
Microwave Semiconductor Devices, H. V. Shurmer (*University of Warwick*)
Physical Electronics, J. Seymour (*Woolwich Polytechnic*)

Further topics proposed are

Electrical Networks
Guided Waves
Electron Devices
Amplifiers and Oscillators
Probability, Noise and Harmonic Analysis
Communication Theory and Information Processing
Communication Systems
Radio Waves
Waveform Generation Techniques
Semiconductor Electronics
Microwave Circuits
Quantum Electronics
Transferred-electron Devices
Ranging Techniques
Automatic Control
Digital Computer Design

Analogue Computer Design
Data Processing
Datal Control using Digital Machines
Telemetry and Data Transmission
Drawing for Electronics
Microcircuit Technology
Television
Electronic Movements
Electronic Techniques in Measurement
Reliability
Mechanical Factors in Electronic Construction
Applied Acoustics
Counting Circuits
Filter Design

Electronic Power Supplies

G. N. PATCHETT
B Sc, Ph D, C Eng, FIEE,
FIERE, MIEEE

*Professor of Electrical Engineering
University of Bradford*

PITMAN PUBLISHING

First Published 1970

SIR ISAAC PITMAN AND SONS LTD
Pitman House, Parker Street, Kingsway, London, WC2B 5PB
P.O. Box 6038, Portal Street, Nairobi, Kenya
SIR ISAAC PITMAN (AUST.) PTY LTD
Pitman House, Bouverie Street, Carlton, Victoria 3053, Australia
PITMAN PUBLISHING COMPANY S.A. LTD
P.O. Box 9898, Johannesburg, S. Africa
PITMAN PUBLISHING CORPORATION
6 East 43rd Street, New York, N.Y. 10017, U.S.A.
SIR ISAAC PITMAN (CANADA) LTD
Pitman House, 381–383 Church Street, Toronto, 3, Canada
THE COPP CLARK PUBLISHING COMPANY
517 Wellington Street, Toronto, 2B, Canada

ISBN 0 273 40079 7

MADE IN GREAT BRITAIN AT THE PITMAN PRESS, BATH
G0—(T.234)

Series Foreword

Professor W. A. Gambling

Electronics (or electronic engineering since the two names are synonymous) is still a rapidly-evolving subject not only in terms of its boundaries, which are still expanding, but also in the techniques being used. For example, active devices have progressed from the electron tube through the bipolar transistor to field-effect devices and integrated circuits, while completely new types such as lasers, transferred-electron diodes and electro-acoustic devices have also emerged. In such a dynamic field it is difficult to keep up with the continually-changing scene and to obtain a modern, authoritative coverage of a topic at an introductory level. The days of the large comprehensive textbook, of which there have been some excellent examples in the past, have gone of course, since the gestation period of a work of this kind is such that it is bound to be out of date before it reaches the bookshelf.

The aim of the present series, therefore, is to produce a number of reasonably concise treatments each covering a specific aspect of electronics. Not only can these be written in a shorter time than can a large book but they are more easily revised and brought up to date. The student (using the term in its broadest sense) can thus select the appropriate volumes to suit the particular aspects of the subject he wishes to cover. Each book is written by a specialist and the academic level in the series as a whole ranges from the early undergraduate stage to postgraduate and professional standard. While potential readers will include both students and young professional engineers the authors have not written with any particular type of examination or teaching syllabus in mind. Indeed some of the titles cover material which students should be aware of but which is not normally classed as "examinable".

Finally a word should perhaps be said about the overall coverage. As stated above, the terms "electronics" and "electronic engineering" mean the same thing and were coined at a time when active devices consisted of electron tubes in which the flow of free electrons is controlled in such a way as to produce amplification of an electrical signal. Nowadays electronics engineers are equally at home using photons, phonons, valence and conduction electrons in solids, electron spin and other quantum states, etc., so that the terms have a less direct meaning than formerly. A better definition comes from a consideration of the function of electronics which is concerned with the transmission, storage, control and processing of information in all its different aspects. A more appropriate title might therefore be "information engineering" although the term "electronics" is now so widely accepted that it is unlikely to be displaced in the near future. In the broad meaning of the term, therefore, electronics involves the processing of information whether it appears in electrical, acoustic, optical or any other form. This is certainly the sense in which it is used in the present series.

Preface

The book is restricted to the description of direct-current electronic power supplies as these are the most common. Unstabilized supplies are first described followed by stabilized constant-voltage supplies using valves or transistors. Constant-voltage constant-current supplies are also considered.

The book is intended for degree and Higher National Diploma and Certificate students who have some knowledge of valves and transistors. However the book should be useful to anyone concerned with the design and/or use of electronic power supplies.

G.N.P.

Contents

1

Introduction

The term *electronic power supply* can cover a very wide range of devices, but in this book it is restricted to small power supplies giving a direct voltage output. It is also assumed that the power supplies are fed from a normal alternating voltage supply. Although the book has been restricted in this way the principles can be applied to power supplies of other types. A stabilized power supply can be split up into sections as shown in Fig. 1.1.

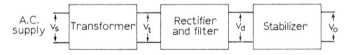

FIG. 1.1 Elements of a stabilized power supply

As the required output voltage is not normally that which would be obtained directly from the mains supply, a transformer is nearly always essential to change the a.c. supply voltage to an appropriate value. The transformer also serves to electrically isolate the mains supply from the output terminals. This is usually essential in the interests of safety and convenience. It is necessary to rectify the output of the transformer to produce an undirectional voltage. Some smoothing will also be required by means of a filter circuit. The rectified supply then feeds the stabilizer, which produces a suitable constant voltage output.

REQUIREMENTS OF AN ELECTRONIC POWER SUPPLY

There are basically two types of power supply—constant voltage and constant current. The former is much more common and important, and for the present this type will be assumed. The main requirement of such a power supply is that it shall produce a constant output voltage. The main causes of voltage variation are

1. Change of input voltage
2. Change of output current or load

Change of Input Voltage

Suppose that the supply voltage is V_s and the output voltage is V_o, and that a change of supply voltage δV_s produces a change of output voltage δV_o, the output current being constant. The stability of the power supply may be expressed as

$$\frac{\text{Change of output voltage, } \delta V_o}{\text{Change of supply voltage, } \delta V_s}$$

This ratio is sometimes known as the *regulation factor*, R_f, and the inverse as the *stabilization ratio*, S. This expression is satisfactory if the supply voltage and output voltage are of approximately the same magnitude but leads to false results if they are not. For example, if V_s and V_o were applied to a transformer with V_o much less than V_s then a change δV_s in the supply voltage would produce a smaller change δV_o in the output voltage, resulting in a regulation factor less than unity and a stabilization ratio greater than unity. A transformer is not considered to be a stabilizing device. There is considerable confusion over this, but the difficulty can be overcome by introducing what will be called the *fractional regulation factor*, R_f', and the *fractional stabilization ratio*, S', defined as follows:

$$\text{Fractional regulation factor, } \frac{\delta V_o}{V_o} \bigg/ \frac{\delta V_s}{V_s}$$

$$\text{Fractional stabilization ratio, } \frac{\delta V_s}{V_s} \bigg/ \frac{\delta V_o}{V_o}$$

In power supply specifications it is not always clear whether stabilization ratio or fractional stabilization ratio is being used. Unfortunately the stability of power supplies is often expressed in various ways, which makes comparison difficult. Sometimes the percentage change of output voltage is quoted for, say, a 10 per cent change in supply voltage. In some ways this is more realistic since most power supplies will only operate over a limited range of supply voltage.

Change of Output Current or Load

It is assumed that the supply voltage remains constant. As the output current of the power supply is increased the output voltage falls and the power supply behaves as if it had an internal resistance. Suppose that a change of output current δI_o produces a change of output voltage δV_o; then the internal or output resistance is given by

$$R_o = -\frac{\delta V_o}{\delta I_o} \text{ ohms}$$

(The minus sign is necessary since an increase in current produces a decrease in voltage; e.g. if δI_o is positive then δV_o is negative.)

If the changes are rapid, being due, for example, to the superimposition of an alternating component on the output current, the above relationship becomes the output impedance, Z_o, and will depend on frequency. Alternatively the percentage decrease in voltage from no load to full load may be quoted.

Other factors which may be important are:

(*a*) *Change of output voltage with change of ambient temperature.* As the ambient temperature changes there is usually some change in output voltage, and this is normally expressed in the form of a temperature coefficient, i.e. percentage change of voltage per degree of temperature change. In some cases the change of ambient temperature may be due to a change of load which changes the dissipation of components.

(*b*) *Ripple and noise.* As the smoothing of a power supply is never perfect there will be some ripple on the output, and this may be expressed as a percentage of the output voltage. Any noise voltage in the output can similarly be expressed.

(*c*) *Response time.* This applies to stabilized power supplies and is not easily defined, and various figures are used. They are considered in more detail later. Any sudden change in input voltage or output current will cause a momentary change of output voltage until the stabilizer circuit has had time to correct it. This time is called the *response time*.

(*d*) *Overload protection or current limiting.* In a stabilized power supply it is usual to have overload protection to prevent damage to the power supply or, in some cases, to the equipment being operated by it. This is discussed in more detail in Chapter 6.

Simple fuse protection is used in unstabilized supplies.

(e) *Overvoltage protection.* When complex transistorized or integrated circuits are fed from a stabilized power supply it is important that the nominal output voltage cannot be exceeded for any cause whatsoever. Suitable circuits are discussed in Chapter 6.

(f) *Output voltage.* This may be fixed, variable over a small range or variable from zero to full voltage. As will be seen later, the particular condition has a considerable influence on design, and the requirement of large variations of output voltage both complicates and increases the cost of a power supply.

(g) *Size and weight.* These may be important in some applications.

(h) *Cost.* This may be a most important factor from the manufacturer's point of view, but is too complex a problem to consider in any detail in this book.

2

Rectification; Unstabilized Power Supplies

It will be assumed that the alternating voltage supply is single phase, and hence the rectifier circuit may be half wave or full wave. As mentioned in Chapter 1 a transformer is normally essential in order to obtain the required output voltage and also in order to isolate the output from the supply. As the output from the rectifier will be an undirectional voltage of varying magnitude some smoothing will normally be necessary. The amount will depend on whether the rectifier is feeding a stabilizer circuit or feeding equipment directly. In the latter case the amount of ripple that can be tolerated will depend greatly on the application. When the rectifier is followed by a stabilizer circuit, considerable ripple is often permissible as the stabilizer itself acts as a smoothing circuit.

HALF-WAVE RECTIFIER CIRCUIT

The basic half-wave rectifier circuit is shown in Fig. 2.1. Transformer T_1 is used to change the supply voltage to a suitable value; Re_1 is the rectifier,

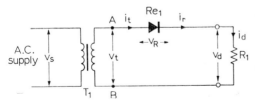

FIG. 2.1 Half-wave rectifier circuit

and R_1 represents the load, i.e. the device being fed from the power supply. It will be assumed that this can be represented by a resistor since operation is considerably more involved if the device is a capacitor, inductor or source of e.m.f. The effect of a capacitor across the load is considered later.

The rectifier Re_1 may be a high-vacuum diode (gasfilled diodes will not be considered), selenium rectifier or semiconductor rectifier, either germanium or silicon.

In a high-vacuum valve the reverse current can be considered to be negligible, but the forward voltage drop is large (say 20–40 V) and approximately proportional to current. The maxium forward current is relatively small (commonly 100 mA mean).

The selenium rectifier has a lower forward voltage drop of about 1 V per element (the value depends on the method of manufacture). The maximum reverse voltage is low (about 20 V, depending on type), and elements are used in series for high voltages resulting in an increased voltage drop in the forward direction. The drop is not proportional to current, little current flowing until a voltage of about 0·3 V is applied. The reverse current is small but rises rapidly with increase in temperature.

Germanium and silicon diodes have similar characteristics, with a forward drop of about 0·5 V for germanium and 1·1 V for silicon. The reverse current of silicon is much smaller than that of germanium and for most purposes can be neglected. The drop is not proportional to current, and it is often convenient to assume that it is independent of current. As the maximum reverse voltage of both types can be high (300 V for germanium, 1 000 V for silicon) they are used in series only on high-voltage supplies. Both are available for large forward currents (100–500 A).

The voltages and currents in the circuit of Fig. 2.1 are shown in Fig. 2.2. At (*a*) is shown the transformer secondary voltage, v_t, which will in all cases be assumed sinusoidal. When point A is positive with respect to B current will flow through the rectifier Re_1 and the load R_1 as shown at (*b*). The magnitude of the current depends on the value of R_1 and on the voltage drop or forward resistance of the rectifier. When B is positive with respect to A, reverse voltage is applied to the rectifier and (assuming a perfect rectifier with negligible reverse current) no current flows. Thus the current consists of half-cycles as shown at (*b*). The half-wave of current will be exactly sinusoidal only if the forward voltage drop of the rectifier is proportional to current. In most cases this is not true and some distortion will occur, the magnitude depending on the non-linearity of the rectifier and on the ratio of rectifier voltage drop to transformer voltage. In general the distortion is small. For convenience it will be assumed that the rectifier drop is proportional to current.

The voltage across the rectifier is shown at (*c*). During the conducting half-cycles the drop is small, but when non-conducting the full transformer

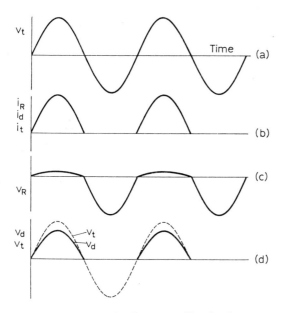

FIG. 2.2 Waveforms of half-wave rectifier circuit

(*a*) Input voltage (voltage of A relative to B)   (*b*) Current in rectifier and load
(*c*) Voltage across rectifier   (*d*) Output voltage

voltage is applied across the rectifier. Thus the rectifier must have a peak inverse voltage (p.i.v.) rating at least equal to the *peak* transformer voltage. The output voltage, v_d (across the load R_1) is shown at (*d*) and is zero during the half-cycles when the transformer voltage, A relative to B, is negative. During the conducting half-cycles the voltage v_d is the transformer voltage, v_t, less the drop, v_R, across the rectifier, as shown.

The disadvantage of the circuit is that the output voltage is zero for half a cycle during each cycle. In general some type of smoothing circuit is necessary to even out or average the voltage.

When dealing with rectifiers it is the mean output voltage that is often

7

quoted, and, of course, the mean output of the half-wave circuit is half the mean value of the half-cycles. Referring to Fig. 2.3, the average of the

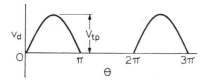

FIG. 2.3 Output waveform of half-wave rectifier circuit neglecting voltage drop in rectifier

half-cycle is

$$\frac{1}{\pi} \int_0^{\pi} V_{tp} \sin \theta \, d\theta = \frac{2}{\pi} V_{tp}$$

where V_{tp} is the peak transformer voltage, or if allowance is made for the rectifier voltage drop, the peak transformer voltage minus the peak rectifier voltage drop. Thus the average output voltage (neglecting the rectifier voltage drop) is

$$V_d' = \frac{V_{tp}}{\pi} = \frac{\sqrt{2}V_t}{\pi} = 0.45V_t \tag{2.1}$$

where V_t is the r.m.s. transformer voltage.

The r.m.s. value of the output voltage, V_d, is the square root of the average value of v_d^2 over the cycle:

$$V_d = \sqrt{\left[\frac{1}{2\pi} \int_0^{\pi} (V_{tp} \sin \theta)^2 \, d\theta\right]}$$

$$= \frac{V_{tp}}{2} = \frac{V_t}{\sqrt{2}} = 0.707V_t \tag{2.2}$$

Therefore the form factor is

$$\frac{\text{R.M.S. value}}{\text{Mean value}} = \frac{V_t}{\sqrt{2}} \frac{\pi}{\sqrt{2}V_t} = \frac{\pi}{2} = 1.57 \tag{2.3}$$

The fact that the output voltage can be expressed either as a mean or an r.m.s. value causes considerable confusion. The mean values of voltage and current are often quoted, but this assumes that before the output is used it is fully smoothed so that the voltage and current are steady. It

$$I = \sqrt{\left[\frac{1}{2\pi} \int_0^\pi (V_{Ep}\, sen\theta)^2 d\theta\right]}$$

$$= \sqrt{\frac{1}{2\pi} \times V_{Ep}^2 \int_0^\pi \left(\frac{1}{2}(1 - \cos 2\theta)d\theta\right)}$$

$$= \sqrt{\frac{V_{Ep}^2}{2\pi}\left(\frac{1}{2}\int_0^\pi d\theta - \frac{1}{2}\int_0^\pi \cos 2\theta\, d\theta\right)}$$

$$= V_{Ep}\sqrt{\frac{1}{2\pi}\left[\frac{1}{2}\theta - \frac{1}{4}\sin 2\theta\right]_0^\pi}$$

$$= V_{Ep}\sqrt{\frac{1}{2\pi}\left[\frac{\pi}{2} - 0 - 0 + 0\right]}$$

$$= V_{Ep}\sqrt{\frac{1}{4}} \qquad = \frac{V_{Ep}}{2}$$

Friday

20

August				
S	1	8	15	22	29
M	2	9	16	23	30
Tu	3	10	17	24	31
W	4	11	18	25	...
Th	5	12	19	26	...
F	6	13	20	27	...
S	7	14	21	28	...

September				
S	...	5	12	19	26
M	...	6	13	20	27
Tu	...	7	14	21	28
W	1	8	15	22	29
Th	2	9	16	23	30
F	3	10	17	24	...
S	4	11	18	25	...

AUGUST, 1971

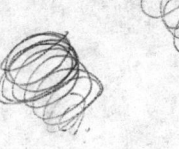

further assumes that there is no loss in the smoothing circuit and that the smoothing circuit does not upset the operation of the rectifier. There must be some loss in the smoothing circuit, and the smoothing circuit normally does alter the operation of the rectifier. If such a circuit is used then the power output is the product of mean voltage and mean current. If a smoothing circuit is not used and, for example, the output is fed to a resistor as shown in Fig. 2.1, the power output is *not* the product of mean voltage and mean current but, of course of r.m.s. voltage and r.m.s. current (provided they are in phase). More accurately it is $I^2 R_1$, where I is the r.m.s. current in the resistor. For the present, therefore, the power output will be taken as the product of r.m.s. voltage and r.m.s. current. This will result in figures which differ from those appearing in other books where the output is taken as the product of mean voltage and mean current.

Without smoothing, the current waveform is similar to the voltage waveform and the same current in the rectifier, load and transformer secondary winding. The r.m.s. value of the current, I_d, is calculated in the same manner as the r.m.s. voltage, and therefore

$$I_d = \frac{I_{dp}}{2} \tag{2.4}$$

where I_{dp} is the peak direct current output.

Thus the output power is

$$P_d = V_d I_d$$

$$= \frac{V_{tp}}{2} \frac{I_{dp}}{2} \text{ (from eqns. (2.2) and (2.4))}$$

$$= \frac{V_{tp} I_{dp}}{4} \tag{2.5}$$

The secondary volt-amperes of the transformer, S_t, will be the product of r.m.s. current and r.m.s. voltage:

$$S_t = \frac{V_{tp}}{\sqrt{2}} \frac{I_{dp}}{2} = \frac{V_{tp} I_{dp}}{2\sqrt{2}} \tag{2.6}$$

Thus

$$\frac{\text{Power output}}{\text{VA rating of secondary}} = \frac{V_{tp} I_{dp}}{4} \frac{2\sqrt{2}}{V_{tp} I_{dp}} \text{ (from eqns. (2.5) and (2.6))}$$

$$= 0 \cdot 707 \tag{2.7}$$

9

Note. In some calculations the current in the rectifier and transformer is assumed to consist of rectangular pulses on the basis of the output current being of constant value, but this is of no practical interest in this case.

This calculation has been done to emphasize the difference between the volt-ampere rating of the transformer and the power output of the rectifier.

If the power dissipation due to reverse current is neglected, the power dissipated in the rectifier is

$$P_R = \frac{1}{2\pi} \int_0^\pi iv \, d\theta$$

$$= \frac{1}{2\pi} \int_0^\pi (I_{dp} \sin \theta)(V_{rp} \sin \theta) \, d\theta$$

$$= \frac{I_{dp} V_{rp}}{4} \tag{2.8}$$

where V_{rp} is the peak rectifier voltage drop.

In the above calculations no allowance has been made for transformer resistance and leakage reactance. The resistance can be allowed for by adding the total effective secondary resistance (i.e. secondary resistance plus primary resistance referred to secondary) to that of the rectifier when considering the output voltage. The effect of leakage reactance is more difficult to compute and will not be considered here.

Another disadvantage of this circuit is that the current flowing in the secondary of the transformer is undirectional (i.e. d.c.), and this causes saturation of the core since a corresponding direct current cannot flow in the primary. The exact operation is rather complex.

This circuit is normally used only where small output current and power are required and for cheapness, e.g. battery charging.

Use of Reservoir Capacitor

In order to overcome the difficulty of zero voltage for half the total time, some type of smoothing circuit is normally required. The simplest method is to connect a reservoir capacitor, C_1, across the output of the rectifier as in Fig. 2.4. The operation of the circuit is now changed considerably, and particularly the operating conditions of the rectifier Re_1.

Consider the circuit switched on at instant 0 in Fig. 2.5. Over the first quarter-cycle OP, point A is positive with respect to B and hence a current will flow through the rectifier. Current will, of course, flow through the load R_1 as previously, but an additional current will be required to charge the capacitor. The output voltage will rise, as at (c), to a maximum (equal to the peak transformer voltage if the rectifier voltage drop is neglected). After point P the transformer voltage drops according to a sine waveform while the voltage across C_1 falls exponentially at a rate determined by the time-constant C_1R_1. As soon as the voltage across C_1 is greater than the

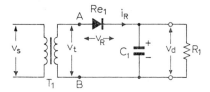

FIG. 2.4 Half-wave rectifier circuit with reservoir capacitor

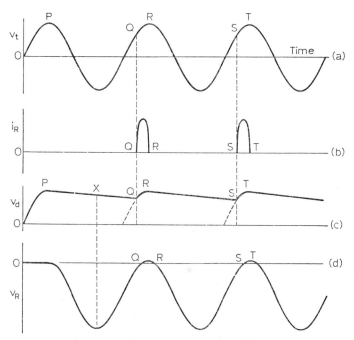

FIG. 2.5 Waveforms of half-wave rectifier circuit with reservoir capacitor

(a) Input voltage (voltage of A relative to B)   (b) Rectifier current
(c) Output voltage   (d) Voltage across rectifier

11

transformer voltage no current flows in Re_1. This condition continues until the transformer voltage again equals the capacitor voltage at point Q. Current now flows in the rectifier, feeding the load R_1 and recharging the capacitor C_1, until point R is reached, when the rectifier voltage is reversed and no current flows. The output voltage waveform is therefore as at (*c*) and a relatively steady output voltage is obtained. The larger the value of C_1 for a given load R_1 (i.e. the larger the time-constant) the less is the drop in voltage between P and Q and the nearer Q moves to R.

Current now flows only through the rectifier as at (*b*). (The initial current flow from 0 to P is not shown as this would be large and is only a transient condition of little importance.) Thus current flows only between Q and R, S and T, etc. Since the mean current through the rectifier must equal the mean current in R_1, the mean value of the waveform (i.e. the area under the curves) at (*b*) must equal the mean current in R_1. Since the current flows for only a short time during each period, the peak value will be much greater than the mean current. The manner in which the current varies between Q and R is similar to that shown, but for simplicity it may be assumed to be a rectangular pulse. Thus, if the interval QR is one-tenth of a cycle then a pulse of current will flow of magnitude 10 times the mean output current in R_1. The longer the time constant $C_1 R_1$ the shorter will be the interval QR and hence the larger the peak current. It is essential that this peak current does not exceed the rating of the rectifier. This same current flows through the transformer secondary and has a high r.m.s. value relative to its mean value, thus increasing the heating in the transformer. The interval QR depends to some extent on the resistance of the rectifier and the effective resistance of the transformer; an increase of such resistance moves point R to the right, and the capacitor does not charge to the peak transformer voltage but to some lower value. A resistor may sometimes be connected in series with the rectifier to limit the peak current.

When B is positive with respect to A it will be seen from Fig. 2.4 that both the transformer voltage and the voltage across C_1 are tending to force current through the rectifier in the reverse direction. The waveform across the rectifier is that shown in Fig. 2.5 (*d*). If the drop from P to Q is small then the voltage across C_1 at point X is approximately the peak transformer voltage, and hence the total voltage applied across the rectifier is approximately twice the peak transformer voltage, although it is rather less on load. If the load is removed then the drop between P and Q becomes negligible and the peak inverse voltage then equals twice the peak transformer voltage. Thus the rectifier must be capable of withstanding a peak inverse voltage equal to *twice* the peak transformer voltage. This is twice the value it has to withstand when a capacitor is not used. Thus the operating conditions are much more severe.

Owing to the high peak rectifier current there is a limit to the amount of smoothing which one can obtain in practice with such a circuit, and commonly the ripple may be 10–30 per cent (i.e. the variation of voltage between P and Q may be 10–30 per cent of the mean output voltage).

The mean direct output voltage is now much greater than without the reservoir capacitor. On no load it becomes equal to the peak transformer voltage, V_{tp}. The ripple and output voltage can be calculated approximately by assuming that Q and R represent the same instant and that PQ is a straight line extending over a cycle, as in Fig. 2.6. Now,

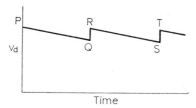

FIG. 2.6 Output voltage ripple in simplified form

$$i = C \frac{dv}{dt}$$

so that

$$\frac{dv}{dt} = \frac{i}{C}$$

which gives the slope of PQ.

For example, consider a 50 Hz supply with a transformer voltage of 25 V (r.m.s.), a load of 1 A mean, and a capacitance of $2\,000\,\mu F$. Then

$$\frac{dv}{dt} = \frac{i}{C} = \frac{1}{2\,000 \times 10^{-6}} = 500 \text{ V/s}$$

The time between P and Q is 1/50, or 0·02 s, and therefore the change of voltage is

$$0 \cdot 02 \frac{dv}{dt} = 0 \cdot 02 \times 500 = 10 \text{ V}$$

13

i.e. the ripple voltage is 10 V peak to peak.

Peak transformer voltage $= \sqrt{2} \times 25 = 35 \cdot 3$ V
The output voltage therefore varies from $35 \cdot 3$ to $35 \cdot 3 - 10 = 25 \cdot 3$ V,

so that

$$\text{Mean voltage, } V_d' = \frac{35 \cdot 3 + 25 \cdot 3}{2} = 30 \cdot 3 \text{ V}$$

and

$$\text{Percentage variation in voltage} = \frac{10}{30 \cdot 3} \times 100 = 33 \text{ per cent}$$

$$\text{Load resistance } R_1 = \frac{V_d'}{I_d'} = \frac{30 \cdot 3}{1} = 30 \cdot 3 \, \Omega$$

The method is often accurate enough in practice, but a more exact calculation can be made by equating the expression for the exponential decrease in voltage from P to Q with that of the sine curve of the transformer voltage to obtain point Q. However, the calculation is difficult if the voltage drop in the rectifier is to be allowed for.

The output voltage of this circuit is proportional to the supply voltage, V_s, and the regulation (variation of voltage with load) or internal resistance is high. In the above example the no-load voltage is $35 \cdot 3$ V (peak transformer voltage) and the voltage at 1 A load is $30 \cdot 3$ V, a drop of $5 \cdot 3$ V. The regulation is therefore $5 \cdot 3/30 \cdot 3 \times 100$, or $17 \cdot 5$ per cent, and the internal resistance is

$$\frac{\text{Change of voltage}}{\text{Change of load current}} = \frac{5 \cdot 3}{1} = 5 \cdot 3 \, \Omega$$

As in the last case the current in the secondary of the transformer will be undirectional and saturation of the transformer core will occur.

It should be noted that the maximum voltage across the capacitor C_1 is the peak transformer voltage. It must therefore be rated for this voltage and not the mean output voltage, since it is subject to this voltage both on load and on no-load. The capacitor is continuously being charged and discharged, or in other words there is an a.c. component or ripple current, as it is usually called, flowing through it. As there are losses in the capacitor, particularly if of the electrolytic variety, it must be designed to carry this current without damage. If, for simplicity, the ripple is assumed sinusoidal of peak value equal to half the variation of voltage, the ripple current can be calculated as follows.

Considering the above example, the variation of voltage is 10 V; hence the equivalent r.m.s. supply voltage is $10/2\sqrt{2}$, or $3\cdot53$ V. The ripple frequency is 50 Hz, so that

$$\text{Ripple current} = \frac{3\cdot53}{\text{Reactance of capacitor}}$$

$$= \frac{3\cdot53}{1/(2\pi \times 50 \times 2\,000 \times 10^{-6})} = 2\cdot22\text{ A}$$

Calculations of the volt-ampere rating of the secondary of the transformer are now more involved. If the ripple is not large then the r.m.s. output voltage will be approximately equal to the mean voltage, and the power will be equal to the square of this voltage divided by the resistance. If the rectifier conduction time is known and the current is assumed to be a rectangular pulse then its r.m.s. value can be calculated in order to find the volt-ampere rating of the transformer secondary.

Owing to the saturation of the transformer core and the greater amount of ripple than with the full-wave circuit, this half-wave circuit is used only at low power levels.

FULL-WAVE RECTIFICATION

In a full-wave rectifier use is made of both half-cycles of the waveform so that the output voltage is zero only instantaneously. Two circuits are commonly used, the centre-tapped transformer circuit and the bridge-rectifier circuit.

The centre-tapped transformer circuit, shown in Fig. 2.7, makes use of two identical rectifiers, Re_1 and Re_2. When point A is positive with respect

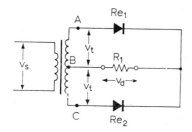

FIG. 2.7 Full-wave rectifier circuit using centre-tapped transformer

15

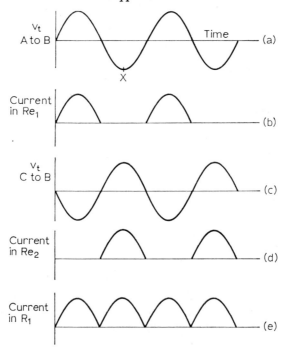

FIG. 2.8 Waveforms of full-wave rectifier circuit

(*a*) Input waveform to rectifier Re$_1$ (*b*) Current in rectifier Re$_1$
(*c*) Input waveform to rectifier Re$_2$ (*d*) Current in rectifier Re$_2$
(*e*) Output current and voltage waveform

to the centre tap B, a current will flow through rectifier Re$_1$ and the load R_1, as shown at (*b*) in Fig. 2.8. During the half-cycle when A is positive with respect to B the voltage at C is negative with respect to B and hence no current flows in Re$_2$, as shown at (*d*). During the next half-cycle the roles are interchanged, current flowing in Re$_2$ (since C is positive with respect to B) and no current flows in Re$_1$. The current which flows in the load R_1 is the sum of the two rectifier currents as shown at (*e*). Essentially the circuit consists of two half-wave rectifiers operating in parallel, their input voltages being 180° out of phase. It may also be considered as a 2-phase circuit, the "phases" being 180° out of phase. Neglecting the drop in the rectifiers the output voltage will be as shown at (*e*), the peak amplitude being equal to the peak magnitude of the transformer voltage, v_t. In practice it will be rather less owing to the drop in the rectifiers.

16

At instant X the voltage trying to send current in the reverse direction through Re_1 is the peak transformer voltage V_{tp} plus the voltage across the load. The latter is equal to the peak transformer voltage if the rectifier drop is neglected. Thus the rectifiers must withstand a peak inverse voltage of twice the peak transformer voltage V_{tp}, this being the voltage of half the winding.

The mean output voltage (neglecting the rectifier drop) is twice that of the half-wave rectifier circuit (see eqn. (2.1)); i.e. the mean output voltage is given by

$$V_d' = \frac{2}{\pi} V_{tp} = 0{\cdot}90 V_t \tag{2.9}$$

where V_{tp} and V_t are the peak and r.m.s. voltages of half the transformer winding.

The r.m.s. value of the output voltage is now given by

$$V_d = \sqrt{\left[\frac{1}{\pi} \int_0^\pi (V_{tp} \sin \theta)^2 \, d\theta \right]} = \frac{V_{tp}}{\sqrt{2}} = V_t \tag{2.10}$$

The output current waveform will be the same as the voltage waveform and its r.m.s. value is calculated in the same way. Thus, the output power is

$$P_d = V_d I_d = \frac{V_{tp}}{\sqrt{2}} \frac{I_{dp}}{\sqrt{2}} = \frac{V_{tp} I_{dp}}{2} \tag{2.11}$$

The secondary volt-amperes of the transformer will be the product of the r.m.s. current and the r.m.s. voltage. The current flowing in each half of the winding consists of one-half cycle per cycle (like a half-wave rectifier) and hence its r.m.s. value is $I_{dp}/2$ (from eqn. (2.4)). The volt-ampere rating of the whole of the secondary winding is therefore

$$S_t = 2 \frac{V_{tp}}{\sqrt{2}} \frac{I_{dp}}{2} = \frac{V_{tp} I_{dp}}{\sqrt{2}} \tag{2.12}$$

Thus

$$\frac{\text{Power output}}{\text{VA rating of secondary}}$$

$$= \frac{V_{tp} I_{dp}}{2} \times \frac{\sqrt{2}}{V_{tp} I_{dp}} \quad \text{(from eqns. (2.11) and (2.12))}$$

$$= 0{\cdot}707 \tag{2.13}$$

as with the half-wave rectifier.

Comparing this circuit with the single-phase circuit, the output voltage is twice as great if the voltage of half the transformer winding is considered but the same value if the total transformer voltage is used. Earlier it was shown that the peak rectifier voltage is $2V_{tp}$, but the output voltage is also double, so in terms of output voltage the rating of each rectifier is the same as in half-wave rectification as regards p.i.v. However two rectifiers are required. The current in each will, of course, be half of that which would flow in a single-phase circuit of the same current output. The ripple is still 100 per cent, but there is no half-cycle when it is zero as in the half-wave rectifier. The ripple frequency is double the frequency of the supply. There is no saturation of the transformer core as the effective current in the total secondary winding is alternating.

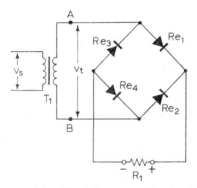

FIG. 2.9 Bridge full-wave rectifier circuit

The bridge rectifier circuit is shown in Fig. 2.9. When point A is positive with respect to B current flows in Re_1, R_1 and Re_4. When B is positive with respect to A then current flows in Re_2, R_1 and Re_3. It will be seen that in both cases the current flows in R_1 in the same direction; hence the waveform will be as in Fig. 2.8 (*e*). Neglecting the rectifier drop, the peak magnitude of the output voltage will equal the peak secondary transformer voltage V_{tp}.

The output voltage V_d' will be as in the centre-tapped transformer circuit (eqn. (2.9)), i.e.

$$V_d' = \frac{2}{\pi} V_{tp} = 0\cdot90V_t$$

but in this case only a single winding of voltage V_t is required.

At the instant when A is most positive with respect to B, the voltage across R_1 will also be of magnitude V_{tp}. Thus the total reverse voltage applied to rectifiers Re_3 and Re_2 in series will be $2V_{tp}$ (i.e. the peak voltage across the transformer plus the voltage across R_1). Hence the p.i.v. rating of *each* rectifier must be V_{tp}, but in practice allowance must be made for inevitable asymmetries in the circuit.

Thus four rectifiers are required of p.i.v. $= V_{tp}$, whereas with the centre-tapped transformer two rectifiers of rating $2V_{tp}$ are required. Thus the "total amount of rectifier" in terms of p.i.v. is the same. The current in the rectifiers consists of half-cycles and is of the same value as in the centre-tapped transformer circuit.

As in the centre-tapped transformer circuit the output power is $P_d = V_{tp}I_{dp}/2$ (eqn. (2.11)). The current flowing in the secondary of the transformer is alterating having a peak value I_{dp} and hence an r.m.s. value $I_{dp}/\sqrt{2}$.

Thus the volt-ampere rating of the transformer secondary is

$$S_t = \frac{V_{tp}}{\sqrt{2}}\frac{I_{dp}}{\sqrt{2}} = \frac{V_{tp}I_{dp}}{2} \qquad (2.14)$$

and

$$\frac{\text{Power output}}{\text{VA rating of secondary}} = \frac{V_{tp}I_{dp}}{2}\frac{2}{V_{tp}I_{dp}} = 1 \qquad (2.15)$$

This is an improvement on the centre-tapped transformer circuit as regards the efficient use of the transformer.

The bridge circuit has the advantage of not requiring a centre-tapped transformer but requires four rectifiers instead of two. The importance of this depends on the type of rectifier. The centre-tapped transformer circuit fits in well with a double-diode valve, as shown in Fig. 2.10, and

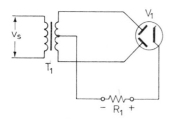

FIG. 2.10 Use of valve as full-wave rectifier with centre-tapped transformer

was at one time almost universally used in electronic equipment. The circuit may also be used with metal or semiconductor diodes. The bridge circuit is difficult, and hence rarely used, with valves since three valves (one being a double diode) and three separate heater supplies are required. It is commonly used with metal rectifiers, the four rectifiers usually being assembled in one unit; it is also used with semiconductor rectifiers.

Use of Reservoir Capacitor

The action of a reservoir capacitor is similar to that explained in connection with the half-wave rectifier. The effect of the capacitor is the same whether a centre-tapped transformer or a bridge circuit is used. The appropriate waveforms are shown in Fig. 2.11. At (*a*) is the input waveform, and at

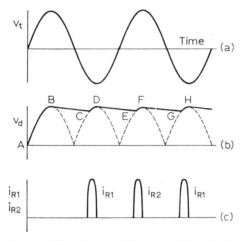

FIG. 2.11 Waveforms of full-wave rectifier circuit with reservoir capacitor

(*a*) Input waveform
(*b*) Output voltage waveform
(*c*) Rectifier current waveform

(*b*), shown dotted, is the output voltage in the absence of a reservoir capacitor.

The capacitor is charged from instant A to instant B (the initial transient condition, of little importance). At B the voltage across the capacitor is greater than the transformer voltage and hence the rectifier becomes non-conducting. The load current is now supplied by the capacitor and the voltage drops from B to C at a rate depending on the time-constant of the circuit. At C the transformer voltage exceeds the capacitor voltage and current flows in the rectifier during the time CD, charging the capacitor. Thus the waveform is as shown by the full line. During the intervals CD, EF and GH current flows in the rectifiers. From C to D and G to H it flows in one rectifier (or one pair in the bridge circuit) and from E to F in the other rectifier (or pair of rectifiers). As in the half-wave circuit the current in the rectifiers consists of pulses of peak magnitude much greater than the average value of the output current. The larger the time-constant the less is the ripple on the output voltage but the shorter are the con-ducting periods and hence the greater is the peak current. Since there are two pulses of current per cycle (instead of the one in the half-wave rectifier), other things being equal the peak current of the full-wave circuit is half that of the half-wave circuit.

In the centre-tapped transformer circuit the transformer secondary current consists of pulses similar to those in a half-wave rectifier, but in the bridge circuit the secondary current consists of pulses in alternate directions as in Fig. 2.12.

Fig. 2.12 Current in secondary of transformer feeding a bridge
rectifier circuit

Since the interval BC is approximately half that of the half-wave circuit (PQ of Fig. 2.5), the magnitude of the ripple of the full-wave circuit is approximately half that of the half-wave circuit. Also the frequency of the ripple is doubled, i.e. the ripple frequency of the full-wave rectifier is twice that of the supply. Calculations of the approximate magnitude of the ripple can be made in the same way as described for the half-wave circuit.

SMOOTHING CIRCUITS

Where the output from the rectifier circuit is used directly rather than through a stabilizer circuit, the smoothing obtained from the use of a reservoir capacitor is often not sufficient. It is therefore necessary to add a smoothing circuit which may be either resistance-capacitance or inductance-capacitance as in Fig. 2.13.

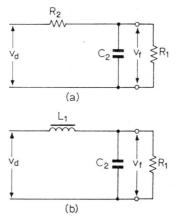

FIG. 2.13 Smoothing circuits
(a) Resistance-capacitance
(b) Inductance-capacitance

The voltage across the reservoir capacitor may be considered as a steady direct voltage (equal to its mean value) plus an alternating component equal to the ripple voltage. The ripple is not, of course, sinusoidal but consists of a fundamental and harmonics. It is usual to consider the fundamental component only, as the filter is more efficient for the harmonics and these are therefore not generally important. As a first approximation the fundamental can be taken to have a peak magnitude equal to the peak magnitude of the ripple.

In Fig. 2.13 (a), capacitor C_2 has an infinite impedance to a direct voltage; thus the circuit consists effectively of two resistors in series and the direct output voltage is V_f'

$$V_f' = \frac{R_1}{R_1 + R_2} V_d'$$

when V_d' is the direct component (or mean value) of the reservoir capacitor voltage. Provided that R_2 is small compared with R_1, most of the rectified voltage appears across the load R_1.

Consider now the a.c. component. If the reactance of C_2 is low compared

22

with R_1 the circuit becomes a simple potential divider circuit as in Fig. 2.14. If the reactance at the ripple frequency of C_2 is X_c then the alternating component of the output voltage is

$$V_f = \frac{X_c}{\sqrt{(R_2{}^2 + X_c{}^2)} V_{da}} \qquad (2.16)$$

where V_{da} is the a.c. component of the rectifier voltage.

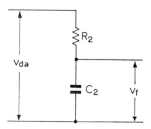

FIG. 2.14 Resistance-capacitance smoothing circuit drawn as potential divider— neglecting load

If X_c can be made small compared with R_2 then the ripple in the output will be much less than that across the reservoir capacitor.

If R_1 cannot be assumed high compared with the reactance of C_2 then the circuit of Fig. 2.15 must be used. The output voltage ripple must now

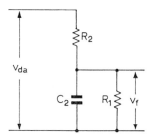

FIG. 2.15 Resistance-capacitance smoothing circuit drawn as potential divider— allowing for load

be expressed in terms of complex quantities:

$$V_f = \frac{Z}{Z + R_2} V_{da} \qquad (2.17)$$

where Z is the impedance of the C_2R_1 parallel circuit. The above expression is solved using normal circuit theory.

Consider an example of a full-wave rectifier supply producing 250 V direct component with 10 per cent peak-to-peak ripple voltage across the reservoir capacitor. Suppose $R_1 = 10\,\text{k}\Omega$, $R_2 = 1\,\text{k}\Omega$ and $C_2 = 32\,\mu\text{F}$. The mains frequency is 50 Hz.

$$\text{Mean output voltage} = \frac{R_1}{R_1 + R_2}V_d' = \frac{10\,000}{10\,000 + 1\,000}250$$

$$= 227\,\text{V}$$

$$\text{Ripple voltage} = \frac{10}{100}250 = 25\,\text{V (p-p)}$$

$$= 12\cdot5\,\text{V (peak)}$$

$$\text{Ripple frequency} = 2 \times \text{mains frequency} = 2 \times 50 = 100\,\text{Hz}$$

$$\text{Reactance of capacitor} = \frac{1}{\omega C} = \frac{10^6}{2\pi \times 100 \times 32} = 49\cdot8\,\Omega$$

This is small compared with R_1 (10 kΩ) and hence, from eqn. (2.16),

$$\text{Output ripple} = \frac{49\cdot8}{\sqrt{(1\,000^2 + 49\cdot8^2)}} \times 12\cdot5 = 0\cdot62\,\text{V(peak)}$$

Thus there is a considerable reduction in the ripple voltage but little reduction in the direct or mean component.

Considering Fig. 2.13 (*b*), if the resistance of L_1 is negligible (compared with R_1) then the direct component of the output voltage is equal to that of the input. This assumption is often true, but if not, and the resistance of L_1 is R_L, then the direct component of the output voltage is

$$V_f' = \frac{R_1}{R_1 + R_L}V_d' \tag{2.18}$$

If the reactance of C_2 at the ripple frequency is low compared with R_1 then the circuit reduces to that of Fig. 2.16 for the alternating component, the resistance of L_1 normally being neglected. If the reactance of L_1 is X_L and that of C_2 is X_c then the ripple in the output is

$$V_f = \frac{X_c}{X_L - X_c}V_{da} \tag{2.19}$$

(This could be a resonant circuit under suitable conditions, but the values are chosen so that it is a long way from resonance, otherwise the ripple might be increased.)

If the reactance of C_2 is not low compared with the load R_1 then the circuit is solved by normal a.c. circuit methods and is most easily done using numerical values rather than by calculating a general formula.

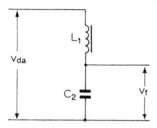

FIG. 2.16 Inductance-capacitance smoothing circuit drawn as potential divider

Consider an example of a 50 Hz supply with a full-wave rectifier. Let $R_1 = 10\,k\Omega$, $L_1 = 10\,H$, $C_2 = 32\,\mu F$ and the resistance of L $(R_L) = 100\,\Omega$. The voltage across the reservoir capacitor is 250 V with 25 V(p-p) ripple. The direct component of the output voltage is

$$V_f' = \frac{R_1}{R_1 + R_L} V_d' = \frac{10\,000}{10\,000 + 100} \times 250 = 247\,V$$

Reactance of $C_2 = 49\cdot9\,\Omega$ (see previous example)

Reactance of $L_1 = \omega L = 2\pi \times 100 \times 10 = 6\,280\,\Omega$

Since the reactance of C_2 is small compared with R_1, the ripple voltage is

$$V_f' = \frac{X_c}{X_L - X_c} V_{da} = \frac{49\cdot8}{6\,280 - 49\cdot8} \times 25$$
$$= 0\cdot2\,V\ (p\text{-}p)$$
$$= 0\cdot1\,V\ (peak)$$

It will be seen that this is much better than the *RC* combination. In general the *RC* circuit is used only when the current is small. It is, of course, much cheaper.

These circuits are commonly used in high-voltage supplies (e.g. 250 V), but in low-voltage supplies it is difficult to construct an inductor with

25

sufficient inductance and a low enough resistance to prevent an excessive voltage drop. For this reason stabilized supplies are commonly used at low voltages as they may be cheaper than a smoothing circuit and also give a constant output voltage.

TYPICAL FIGURES

In all cases the fractional stabilization ratio will be approximately unity, i.e. the output voltage will change by the same percentage as the percentage change of input voltage. The regulation of the power supply will depend on the size of the reservoir capacitor and the resistance of the smoothing inductor, etc.

Supply	No-load voltage	Full-load voltage	Regulation	Internal resistance
250 V 50 mA:	V	V	%	Ω
selenium rectifiers	350	226	55	2 500
30 V 1 A: silicon rectifiers*				
half wave	36	26	39	10
full wave	36	29	24	7

* No smoothing circuit; only a reservoir capacitor.

3

General Principles of Stabilized Power Supplies

MEASURING UNIT AND REGULATING UNIT

In order to maintain a constant output voltage from a power supply two basic devices are necessary: what will be termed a *measuring unit* and a *regulating unit*. The purpose of the measuring unit is to detect any departure in output voltage (or current, if it is a current stabilizer) from its correct value. This then feeds a signal to the regulating unit, which makes the necessary correction to the output. This is most easily explained in terms of a constant-voltage power supply, but the principles apply equally to a constant-current supply, and such supplies will be considered later. For the stabilized supplies being considered in this book, the regulating unit may be placed in one of two positions and the measuring unit in one of three positions.

POSITION OF MEASURING UNIT

The three positions in which the measuring unit may be placed are as shown in Fig. 3.1, namely (a) across the input, (b) across the output, or (c) in series with the output. In this diagram only one of the two possible positions of the regulating unit is shown. In order to explain the operation of these arrangements a factor called the *regulator amplification*, M, is introduced, this being given by

$$M = \frac{\text{Change of voltage across regulating unit}}{\text{Change of voltage across measuring unit}} = \frac{\delta V_{RU}}{\delta V_{MU}}$$

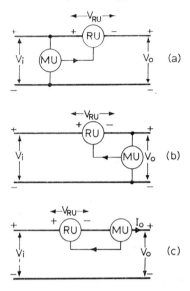

FIG. 3.1 Positions of measuring unit in voltage stabilizer

(*a*) Across input
(*b*) Across output
(*c*) In series with load

MEASURING UNIT ACROSS INPUT

Consider Fig. 3.1 (*a*), where a change of input voltage δV_i occurs which results in a change of output voltage δV_o. From the circuit,

$$\delta V_o = \delta V_i - \delta V_{RU} \tag{3.1}$$

where δV_{RU} is the change of voltage across the regulating unit.

From the definition of regulator amplification, M, $\delta V_{RU} = M \delta V_{MU}$, and substituting in eqn. (3.1),

$$\delta V_o = \delta V_i - M \delta V_{MU}$$

But $\delta V_{MU} = \delta V_i$, since the measuring unit is connected across the input. Thus

$$\delta V_o = \delta V_i - M \delta V_i$$

or

$$\frac{\delta V_o}{\delta V_i} = 1 - M \tag{3.2}$$

where $\delta V_o / \delta V_i$ is the regulation factor, R_f.

If M is made equal to unity then the regulation factor becomes zero and the output voltage is independent of changes of input voltage.

Although this may sound ideal the arrangement suffers from two disadvantages:

(*a*) If R_f is to be zero then M must be exactly unity. If M changes by 10 per cent to 0·9 then R_f becomes $1 - 0·9 = 0·1$ and the performance is poor. For ideal operation M must be exactly unity and must not vary with ambient temperature, ageing, etc. It is impossible to satisfy this condition in practice.

(*b*) Changes in load current will cause changes in output voltage since the regulating unit will have some internal resistance. Since changes of current do not influence the measuring unit, no correction is made for load changes.

For these reasons this arrangement is rarely used on its own. It is, in fact, an open loop control system.

MEASURING UNIT ACROSS OUTPUT

Consider the circuit of Fig. 3.1 (*b*).

As previously,

$$\delta V_o = \delta V_i - \delta V_{RU}$$

and

$$\delta V_{RU} = M \delta V_{MU}$$

but now the measuring unit is across the output, and hence

$$\delta V_{MU} = \delta V_o$$

Thus

$$\delta V_o = \delta V_i - M \delta V_{MU} = \delta V_i - M \delta V_o$$

or

$$\frac{\delta V_o}{\delta V_i} = \frac{1}{1 + M} \tag{3.3}$$

The regulation factor is now made small by making M large, but it cannot be made zero without making M infinite. In spite of this disadvantage the regulation factor is not critically dependent on M as in the last case.

For example, suppose $M = 500$. Then

$$R_f = \frac{1}{1 + 500} = 0.002$$

Now suppose M changes by 10 per cent to 450; then

$$R_f = \frac{1}{1 + 450} = 0.002\,2$$

and the stabilization is almost as good as previously. Compare with the last case, where the change was from 0 to 0·1.

Correction now takes place whatever the reason for the change of output voltage, i.e. the stabilizer corrects for changes of both input voltage and load current. For the above reasons this arrangement is almost always used.

Readers will probably realize that this arrangement is really a negative-feedback amplifier and that M is the loop gain.

MEASURING UNIT IN SERIES WITH OUTPUT

For the arrangement of Fig. 3.1 (c) the definition of M has to be modified since the measuring unit is detecting changes of current and not voltage. Thus

$$M = \frac{\text{Change of voltage across regulating unit}}{\text{Change of current in measuring unit}} = \frac{\delta V_{RU}}{\delta I_o}$$

The circuit has been redrawn in Fig. 3.2, where a resistance R has been added to represent the internal resistance of the regulating unit.

$$\delta V_o = \delta V_i - \delta I_o R + \delta V_{RU}$$

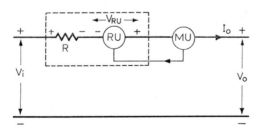

FIG. 3.2 Effect of measuring unit in series with load

If the input voltage V_i is assumed constant, then

$$\delta V_o = -\delta I_o R + \delta V_{RU}$$

But $\delta V_{RU} = M \delta I_o$; hence

$$\delta V_o = -\delta I_o R + M \delta I_o$$

or

$$\frac{\delta V_o}{\delta I_o} = M - R$$

The effective internal resistance is

$$R_i = -\frac{\delta V_o}{\delta I_o}$$

the minus sign being required because an increase of I_o results in a decrease in V_o. Hence

$$R_i = R - M \tag{3.4}$$

Thus if M is made equal to R (note that M has the dimensions of resistance) then the internal resistance $R_i = 0$. The arrangement has similar disadvantages to the circuit of Fig. 3.1 (*a*) but may be used in conjunction with the circuit of Fig. 3.1 (*b*) as explained later.

MEASURING UNIT ACROSS INPUT AND OUTPUT

If the circuits of Figs. 3.1 (*a*) and (*b*) are combined the advantages of both arrangements are obtained as regards change of input voltage. Suppose the regulator amplification of the measuring unit across the input is M_i and that across the output is M_o, and that both feed a common regulating unit. From eqn. (3.1),

$$\delta V_o = \delta V_i - \delta V_{RU}$$

But

$$\delta V_{RU} = \delta V_i M_i + \delta V_o M_o$$

Hence

$$\delta V_o = \delta V_i - \delta V_i M_i - \delta V_o M_o$$

and

$$R_f = \frac{\delta V_o}{\delta V_i} = \frac{1 - M_i}{1 + M_o} \tag{3.5}$$

31

Thus any error due to M_i not being unity is divided by $1 + M_o$, which can be made large.

MEASURING UNITS ACROSS OUTPUT AND IN SERIES WITH LOAD

In a similar way, if the circuits of Figs. 3.1 (*b*) and (*c*) are combined, the internal resistance is given by

$$R_i = \frac{R - M_s}{1 + M_o} \tag{3.6}$$

where M_s = Regulator amplification of measuring unit in series with output

M_o = Regulator amplification of measuring unit across output

Again any error due to M_s not being equal to R is divided by the factor $1 + M_o$, and if $1 + M_o$ is large, good performance is obtained for change of output voltage due to change of current.

MEASURING UNITS ACROSS INPUT, ACROSS OUPUT AND IN SERIES WITH LOAD

Three measuring units may be used (i.e. a combination of Figs. 3.1 (*a*), (*b*) and (*c*), resulting in good performance for both input voltage and load current changes, i.e. small regulation factor R_f and small internal resistance R_i.

POSITION OF REGULATING UNIT

The two possible positions of the regulating unit are given in Fig. 3.3, only one possible position of the measuring unit being shown. At (*a*) the regulating unit is in series with the load, while at (*b*) it is in parallel with load together with a series resistor R_s. In both these cases the regulating unit will dissipate the excess power (a special case where this is not true is covered in Chapter 7). In (*a*) the power in the regulating unit is $(V_i - V_o)I_o$ and is a maximum under conditions of maximum load current (other factors being constant). Provided that the output voltage is not much less than the input voltage, the power to be dissipated in the regulating unit can be much less than the output power of the stabilizer.

Consider an example of a 50 V 1 A supply where the input voltage is 60 V ± 10 per cent. The maximum dissipation occurs when the input voltage is a maximum, i.e. 66 V, and the current is a maximum. It is then $(66 - 50)1 = 16$ W, whereas the output power is $50 \times 1 = 50$ W.

In Fig. 3.3 (*b*) the output voltage is maintained constant by varying the current through the regulating unit. If the input voltage increases then the current in the regulating unit must increase, so that the increase in voltage drop across the series resistor R_s just equals the increase in input voltage. If the load current changes, the current in the regulating unit must change by the same amount so that the current in R_s and the drop across it remain constant.

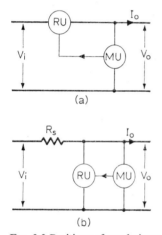

(a)

(b)

FIG. 3.3 Positions of regulating unit

(*a*) In series with load
(*b*) Across output together with series resistor R_s.

If the same power supply is considered but with a nominal input voltage of 75 V then the normal drop across R_s is 25 V. When the input voltage is a minimum, i.e. $75 - 7 \cdot 5 = 67 \cdot 5$ V (75 V − 10 per cent), the drop across R_s is 17·5 V. The resistance R_s is therefore 17·5 Ω assuming under these conditions that the load is 1 A and that no current flows in the regulating unit. When the input voltage is a maximum, i.e. $75 + 7 \cdot 5 = 82 \cdot 5$ V, the drop across R_s is 32·5 V. For the same output voltage the current in R_s must now be $32 \cdot 5 / 17 \cdot 5 = 1 \cdot 86$ A, and assuming the same load current, the current in the regulating unit is 0·86 A. Thus if the load were constant at 1 A the regulating unit would have to dissipate $0 \cdot 86 \times 50 = 43$ W at

33

maximum input voltage and nothing at minimum input voltage. Under the conditions of maximum input voltage and zero load current (the worst conditions as regards the regulating unit) the current in R_s must still be 1·86 A, and all this current must be passed by the regulating unit.

The maximum regulating unit dissipation is therefore $1·86 \times 50 = 93$ W. This is greater than the maximum output power (50 W) and much greater than that calculated for the case of the regulating unit in series with the load (16 W). Obviously the exact figures will depend on the voltages used, but for Fig. 3.3 (*b*) the dissipation of the regulating unit must be greater than that of the load if the stabilizer is to operate down to zero load. It is important to note that in this arrangement the maximum dissipation in the regulating unit occurs at no load (or minimum load), whereas it is a maximum for Fig. 3.3 (*a*) under conditions of maximum load. Circuit (*b*) has the advantage that a short-circuit of the load does not overload the regulating unit, whereas in circuit (*a*) a short-circuit of the load causes full voltage to be applied to the regulating unit with a current equal to the short-circuit current. Since the dissipation of the regulating unit (for a given output) is less in circuit (*a*) than in circuit (*b*), circuit (*a*) is more commonly used, but circuit (*b*) is sometimes used for low powers. Some method of protecting the regulating unit in circuit (*a*) from the effects of overload and short-circuit is essential and is considered later.

CONSTANT CURRENT STABILIZERS

When a constant-current power supply is required the principles remain the same except that a measuring unit is required which detects changes of current. In practice it does not normally detect changes of current directly but measures the changes of voltage across a series resistor. This is shown in Fig. 3.4, where R is the series resistor and R_L is the load resistor. Any

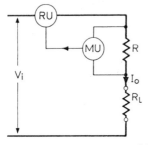

Fɪɢ. 3.4 Constant-current stabilizer circuit

variation of load current I_o will cause variations of voltage across R and hence in the voltage fed to the measuring unit. This causes an appropriate change in current so that the voltage across R is maintained constant. In this diagram the regulating unit is connected in series with the load as this is the normal position.

As the value of R_L is increased the voltage across it rises (since the current through it is constant), and protective circuits may be used to prevent this becoming excessive. There are also some limitations in the regulating unit, which also must be protected.

4

Constant Voltage Sources

In stabilized power supplies a reference voltage is required with which the output voltage can be compared in the measuring unit. In this chapter possible reference voltage sources will be considered.

BATTERIES

The most obvious source of voltage is a battery of some type, and at one time dry batteries were commonly used. Batteries suffer the disadvantage of requiring renewal from time to time. The constancy of the voltage of a dry battery is good under no-load conditions and figures of 0·05 per cent over a three-month period are quoted (Reference 1). The temperature coefficient of voltage is about 0·02 %/°C.

An alternative to the dry battery is a standard cell, which has excellent stability but rather a high temperature coefficient (about $-40\,\mu\text{V}/°\text{C}$ for saturated cells). A standard cell has the disadvantage that its voltage is low. Such cells may, of course, be connected in series but they are expensive and relatively large.

Mainly because of their inconvenience, batteries are little used at the present time.

NON-LINEAR DEVICES

Instead of using an actual constant voltage source a non-linear device may be used to provide an almost constant voltage from a rectified supply voltage.

Two devices are used, namely the cold-cathode discharge valve, and the Zener diode. The former is used in high-voltage stabilizers (say above

150 V) and was very common at one time. It is now tending to be replaced by the Zener diode, which is used in all low-voltage power supplies.

As shown in Fig. 4.1, over a portion AB the two devices have similar

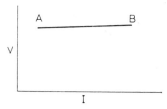

FIG. 4.1 Basic characteristic of cold-cathode discharge tube and Zener diode

characteristics; i.e. over a range of current the voltage is approximately constant, independent of the current. Either of the devices, D, is connected as in Fig. 4.2, the current being limited by the resistor *R*.

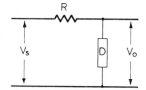

FIG. 4.2 Simple stabilizing circuit using device with characteristic shown in Fig. 4.1

The operating point may be determined by plotting the characteristic as in Fig. 4.3, together with the load line, the point of intersection, X,

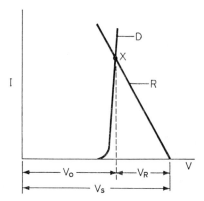

FIG. 4.3 Operation of stabilizer circuit of Fig. 4.2

giving the operating point. The load line is drawn from the point corresponding to the supply voltage. The voltage output (i.e. that across the non-linear device D) is given by V_o and that across the resistor by V_R. If the supply voltage, V_s, varies then the point of intersection moves up and down the characteristic curve of D but little change of V_o results.

If the characteristic is assumed linear as in Fig. 4.4 then the voltage is

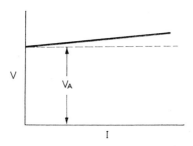

Fig. 4.4 Simplified characteristic of cold-cathode discharge tube or Zener diode

given by

$$V = V_A + IR_i$$

where R_i is the slope resistance of the device, and V_A is the intercept on the voltage axis. Thus, from the point of view of fluctuations or the a.c. component, the circuit becomes as in Fig. 4.5.

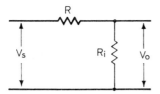

Fig. 4.5 Equivalent circuit of stabilizer circuit for voltage variations

$$\frac{\text{Change of output voltage}}{\text{Change of input voltage}} = \frac{R}{R + R_i}$$

So that, provided R_i is small compared with R, the fluctuations of output voltage will be small compared with those of input voltage.

The two devices will now be considered in more detail.

COLD-CATHODE DISCHARGE VALVE

This consists basically of two electrodes in an inert gas and operated so that a glow discharge takes place between the electrodes. The voltage drop depends on the material of the electrodes and the gas filling and varies from 70 to 150 V. The constant voltage characteristic only obtains over a limited range of current, and the device may become unstable at low currents and is damaged by excessive current. In order to start the discharge a voltage greater than the running voltage must be applied, commonly 30 per cent greater. Discharge valves vary greatly in their characteristics, particularly as regards their stability, and care is necessary in choice if high stability is required. Two general types are manufactured: regulator tubes designed to deal with considerable power, and reference tubes of limited power-handling ability but designed for good stability. A lot of work has been done on the stability of discharge tubes (Refs. 2–9), and modern tubes are much better than earlier types. There is a tendency for the voltage to change for no apparent reason, and the stability generally improves with continuous running.

The discharge tube is still used in certain applications (mainly high-voltage power supplies) but is gradually being replaced by the Zener diode. The minimum voltage of 70 V is too high for low-voltage power supplies, and Zener diodes are smaller, more stable and available for a wide range of voltages.

ZENER DIODE

The Zener diode is a silicon diode, and at low reverse voltages the reverse current is very small. At a certain reverse voltage, however, the current increases rapidly and only a slight change of voltage is required to produce a large change of current. Put in another way, large changes of current produce only small changes of voltage. A typical characteristic is shown in Fig. 4.6.

The voltage at which the sudden increase of current occurs is known as the *Zener voltage* or *breakdown voltage*. It is important to note that this does not imply a breakdown like insulation breakdown, as the characteristic is reproducible and no damage is done by operating in this region.

Zener diodes are so called because it was thought at first that the phenomenon of breakdown was that proposed by Zener, but this is true only for diodes operating below about 5 V; they are sometimes called *field-effect Zener diodes.* Breakdown of the high-voltage types is thought to be due to avalanche multiplication, and hence they may be called *avalanche diodes.* It will be seen that there are significant differences in the characteristics of the two types.

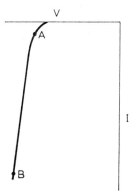

FIG. 4.6 Reverse characteristic of Zener diode

In a similar way to the discharge valve, a Zener diode may be used as a low-power constant-voltage source or as a reference voltage source. In the former case the diode must handle appreciable power and stability

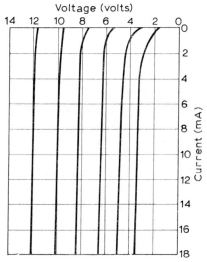

FIG. 4.7 Typical reverse characteristics of Zener diodes

is not of first importance. When the diode is used as a reference voltage source the power in the circuit is reduced and long-term stability is most important.

Zener diodes are available with Zener voltages from about 3 V to several hundred volts, but commonly up to about 50 V. A set of characteristics is shown in Fig. 4.7, where it will be seen that the change from the non-conducting to the conducting state takes place more abruptly the higher the Zener voltage. It is often convenient to assume that over the portion AB (Fig. 4.6) the characteristic is straight and can be expressed by the equation

$$V = V_A + IR_t$$

where V_A is the intercept on the voltage axis and R_i is the slope resistance. In practice the characteristic is more complex and the slope resistance varies with current. The manner in which the slope resistance varies with Zener voltage and current is shown in Fig. 4.8, where it will be seen that for any

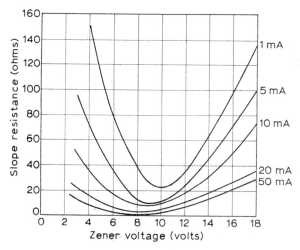

Fig. 4.8 Typical slope resistances of Zener diodes

particular diode the greater the current the lower is the slope resistance. It will also be seen that the minimum slope resistance occurs at 8–9 V, depending to some extent on the value of current.

It is now important to consider the design of a suitable circuit, the basic circuit being as in Fig. 4.9, where the Zener diode is represented by a battery of voltage V_A together with a resistance R_i representing its slope resistance. Many expressions have been worked out for the design of such a circuit, but several are useless since R_i is far from constant and large errors result if it is assumed constant. It would appear that the only method of design and calculation of performance is by using the actual slope resistance of the Zener diode at the particular current concerned. Numerical examples will therefore be considered.

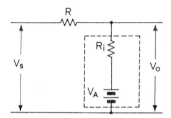

FIG. 4.9 Equivalent circuit of Zener-diode stabilizer circuit

A 12 V Zener diode (at normal current) is operated from a supply of 20 V. A current of 10 mA will be assumed. The voltage across the series resistor R will be $20 - 12 = 8$ V, and hence $R = 8/0\cdot01 = 800\,\Omega$. Using Fig. 4.8, a typical slope resistance at 10 mA is $20\,\Omega$. Consider a change of output voltage of $0\cdot01$ V. For this change the current in the diode must change by $0\cdot01/20 = 0\cdot000\,5$ A. This change of current also takes place in the series resistor causing a change of voltage across it of $0\cdot000\,5 \times 800 = 0\cdot4$ V. Thus the change of input voltage equals the change of voltage across the Zener diode plus the change of voltage across R, i.e. $0\cdot01 + 0\cdot4 = 0\cdot41$ V. Thus the regulation factor, R_f, is $0\cdot01/0\cdot41 = 0\cdot024\,4$, and the fractional regulation factor, R_f', is

$$\frac{\dfrac{0\cdot01}{12}}{\dfrac{0\cdot41}{20}} = \frac{0\cdot01}{12} \times \frac{20}{0\cdot41} = 0\cdot040\,7$$

It might be suggested that the performance would be improved by increasing the value of R. Suppose R is doubled to $1\,600\,\Omega$, other factors being the same. The voltage across R is still 8 V and hence the current is $8/1\,600 = 5$ mA. Using Fig. 4.8, a typical slope resistance at this current is $26\,\Omega$. Thus the change of current for a $0\cdot01$ V change of output voltage is $0.01/26 = 0.000\,385\,A$. The change of voltage across R is now $0.000\,385 \times 1\,600 = 0.616\,V$; and the change of input voltage is $0.01 + 0.616 = 0.626$. The regulation factor is $0.01/0.626 = 0.016$, so that the fractional regulation factor is

$$\frac{0.01}{12} \times \frac{20}{0.626} = 0.026\,6$$

It is seen that increasing the value of R does improve the performance, but the change of slope resistance tends to offset the improvement.

Improved performance is obtained when R is increased if the current is maintained constant by increasing the input voltage. If R is doubled then the drop across R is doubled to $16\,V$ and the supply voltage becomes $12 + 16 = 28\,V$. As in the first case, a change of $0.01\,V$ in the output voltage causes a change of current of $0.000\,5\,A$. The change of voltage across R is now $0.000\,5 \times 1\,600 = 0.80\,V$; and the change of input voltage is $0.01 + 0.80 = 0.81\,V$. The regulation factor, R_f, is $0.01/0.81 = 0.124$. This is practically half that of the first case, but this figure can be misleading and the fractional regulation factors should be compared. In this case,

$$R_f' = \frac{0.01}{12} \times \frac{28}{0.81} = 0.028\,8$$

Thus there is an improvement but not as great as might be expected.

Greatly improved performance can be obtained by using two Zener diodes in cascade as in Fig. 4.10. For a fair comparison the original

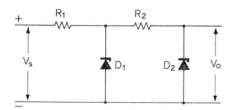

FIG. 4.10 Cascade Zener diode stabilizer circuit

figures will be used, i.e. $V_s = 20\,V$, $V_o = 12\,V$ and current in $D_2 = 10\,mA$. Suppose that the voltage of D_1 is $16\,V$. The voltage across R_2 is therefore $16 - 12 = 4\,V$ and its value is $4/0.01 = 400\,\Omega$. It will be assumed that the current in D_1 is also $10\,mA$, and hence the current in R_1 is $20\,mA$. The voltage across R_1 is $4\,V$ and hence $R_1 = 4/0.02 = 200\,\Omega$.

As previously, a change of output voltage of 0·01 V will result in a change of current in D_2 and R_2 of 0·000 5 A. Thus the change of voltage across R_2 is 0·000 5 × 400 = 0·20 V, and the change of voltage across D_1 is 0·01 + 0·20 = 0·21 V. From Fig. 4.8, a typical slope resistance of a 16 V Zener diode at a current of 20 mA is 30 Ω. For a voltage change of 0·21 V across D_1, the current must change by 0·21/30 = 0·007 A. Thus the total change of current in R_1 is 0·007 + 0·000 5 = 0·007 5 A. This results in a change of voltage of 0·007 5 × 200 = 1·5 V. The input voltage change is therefore 1·50 + 0·21 = 1·71 V. The regulation factor, R_f, is 0·01/1·71 = 0·005 85, and the fractional regulation factor is

$$R_f' = \frac{0·01}{12} \times \frac{20}{1·71} = 0·009\,76$$

This is a considerable improvement on the simple case, which gave a regulation factor of 0·024 4 and a fractional regulation factor of 0·040 7. Obviously the exact performance will depend on the values of the resistors chosen and the slope resistances of the Zener diodes. Since the diode slope resistance changes with current no simple mathematical calculation can be used to get an optimum result. The optimum can only be arrived at by trial and error.

The effects of changes of load have not been considered, since if the Zener diode is used to produce a reference voltage the change will normally be small, but there are exceptions.

It should be noted from Fig. 4.8 that, if the required reference voltage exceeds about 15 V, the slope resistance may be reduced by using lower-voltage Zener diodes in series rather than a single diode. For example a 16 V Zener diode at 10 mA has a slope resistance of 53 Ω, whereas an 8 V Zener diode has a slope resistance of 10 Ω and two would have a value of 20 Ω. It will be seen later that this may also reduce the change of voltage due to temperature.

The slope resistance so far considered is that due to a superimposed alternating current at, say 50 Hz. If the frequency is made very low, say a few cycles per minute, then a different value of slope resistance may be obtained. This is because the temperature of the diode will change during the cycle, and since it has a temperature coefficient, there will be a change of voltage due to the change of temperature. If there is a sudden change of current through a Zener diode then there will be a sudden change of voltage determined by the slope resistance (as measured at 50 Hz) followed by a slow change as the temperature changes. This is shown in Fig. 4.11.

The later change of voltage may be an increase or a decrease depending on whether the Zener diode has a negative temperature coefficient (below about 5 V) or a positive temperature coefficient (above about 5 V). This slow change of voltage may be troublesome. In some circuits it is possible to compensate for the *a.c. slope resistance*, but this then leaves this slow change in voltage due to change of temperature. The slope resistance which

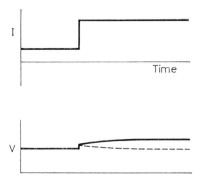

FIG. 4.11 Effect of change of temperature with load change on Zener diode circuit

takes into account the change of temperature is sometimes called the *d.c. slope resistance* (not to be confused with the d.c. resistance). The difference between the a.c. and d.c. slope resistances may be large and care must be taken as to which is used.

Effect of Temperature on the Voltage of a Zener Diode: Temperature Coefficient

Unfortunately, as already mentioned, the voltage of a Zener diode changes with temperature. Diodes which have a Zener voltage below about 5 V (field-effect diodes) have a negative temperature coefficient which increases as the voltage decreases. Diodes which have Zener voltages above about 5 V (avalanche diodes) have a positive temperature co-efficient, and this increases with increase of voltage. The manner in which the temperature coefficient changes with Zener voltage is shown in Fig. 4.12. The temperature coefficient does depend on current, but the current does not have much effect if the Zener voltage is around 7 V. It is seen that the temperature coefficient is zero for diodes with a Zener voltage of

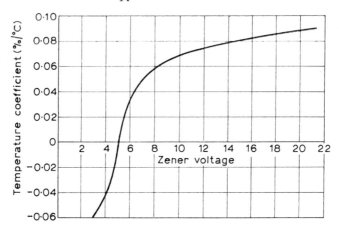

Fig. 4.12 Temperature coefficients of Zener diodes for constant current

about 5 V. However, the temperature coefficient does vary with the current in the Zener diode and the actual ambient temperature. This is apparent from Fig. 4.13, which shows the change of voltage with temperature for various values of current. It will be seen that the temperature coefficient is exactly zero only at one particular temperature and current.

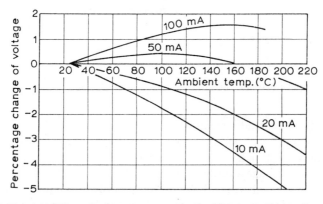

Fig. 4.13 Effect of temperature on voltage of Zener diode at various currents

In the diagram the temperature coefficient is small for a current of 50 mA. It is possible by suitable choice of current to obtain almost zero temperature coefficients for Zener voltages between 5 and 6 V. Rather than state the temperature coefficient it is better to quote the actual change of voltage between two temperatures for a constant and stated current.

For voltages above 5 V it is seen that the temperature coefficient rises rapidly at first but then becomes approximately constant. If a Zener voltage higher than 5 V is required with a low temperature coefficient then a number of 5 V Zener diodes may be used in series.

An alternative method is to use a higher-voltage Zener diode in series with one or more forward-biased Zener diodes or ordinary silicon diodes. In the forward direction the voltage drop is about 0·7 V and the change of voltage with temperature is about 2 mV/°C. Suppose that a 9 V Zener diode is used with a temperature coefficient of 0·068 per cent/°C. A 1°C rise in temperature will cause an increase in voltage of 0·068 × 9/100 = 6 mV. Thus if three forward-biased diodes are used, each with a temperature change of 2 mV/°C, the resultant temperature coefficient will be zero. In practice it will only be zero at one temperature and one current but obviously will be much smaller than that of an uncompensated diode.

A number of commercial reference devices using this idea are manufactured, and very low temperature coefficients such as 0·005%/°C are quoted. The temperature coefficient is normally very dependent on the current and hence the device must be operated at a constant current of the correct value. The references device should therefore be preceded by a constant-voltage circuit such as that in Fig. 4.14. The voltage is

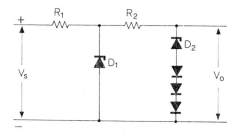

FIG. 4.14 Use of forward biased diodes for temperature compensation, and of constant-voltage circuit to feed reference-diode circuit

stabilized by Zener diode D_1 together with R_1. The almost constant voltage across D_1 causes an approximately constant current to flow in R_2 and reference device D_2. More complex constant-current circuits may be used.

Cancellation of Slope Resistance

It has been shown that, although the slope resistance of a Zener diode is small, it is not negligible. However, it is possible to compensate for it, and a suitable circuit is shown in Fig. 4.15, where D is the Zener diode with a slope resistance R_i.

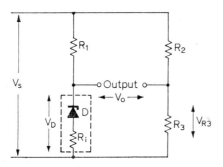

FIG. 4.15 Method of compensation for slope resistance of Zener diode

For changes of input voltage the change of voltage across the Zener diode is given by

$$\delta V_D = \delta V_s \frac{R_i}{R_1 + R_i}$$

where δV_s is the change of input voltage. The change of voltage across R_3 is given by

$$\delta V_{R3} = \delta V_s \frac{R_3}{R_2 + R_3}$$

There will be no change of voltage across the output if these two changes are equal, i.e. if

$$\frac{R_i}{R_1 + R_i} = \frac{R_3}{R_2 + R_3}$$

and there is generally no difficulty in satisfying this condition. This compensation will hold over only a small range of current since R_i is dependent on current. This circuit can only compensate for the a.c. slope resistance. Slow changes due to changes in temperature, due to changes in dissipation, cannot be compensated for. The circuit has the disadvantage that neither of the output connections is common with an input connection.

5

Valve Stabilizer Circuits

Although they have been replaced by transistors in many applications, valves are still used in high-voltage stabilizer circuits, since high-voltage transistors are expensive and are not available for use at voltages above about 300 V. A number of open-loop voltage stabilizer circuits are possible, but only closed-loop control circuits will be considered here. The most common arrangement, shown in Fig. 5.1, consists of a measuring unit

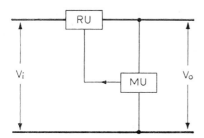

FIG. 5.1 Common basic stabilizer circuit used with valves

across the output and a regulating unit in series with the supply. In some cases the regulating unit is connected across the output together with a series resistor, but this alternative will not be considered. In the measuring unit the output voltage, V_o, or a fraction of it, is compared with a constant voltage source such as a battery or discharge valve. The error voltage is fed to the regulating unit through a d.c. amplifier, the regulating unit consisting of a triode or pentode.

A simple circuit is given in Fig. 5.2. The reference voltage is obtained from across the discharge valve V_3, which is fed from the input through resistor R_4. A potential divider R_1, R_2 is connected across the output, and the values of R_1 and R_2 are chosen so that, at the correct output voltage, the voltage across R_2 is approximately the same as that across the discharge valve V_3. Any difference is applied between the grid and cathode of the amplifier valve V_1. The amplifier output across the load resistor R_3 is fed to the series triode V_2. Thus, if the output voltage tends to increase (owing, say, to an increase of input voltage, V_i), the voltage across R_2 increases so making the grid less negative with respect to the cathode (i.e. the grid voltage goes in a positive direction with respect to the cathode).

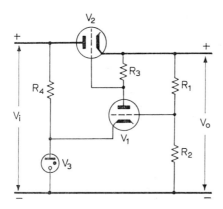

FIG. 5.2 Typical valve stabilizer circuit

This causes an increase in anode current so that the anode voltage of V_1 decreases thus making the grid of V_2 more negative with respect to its cathode. This increases the effective resistance of V_2 so tending to lower the output voltage and correct the error. When equilibrium conditions have been reached the output voltage must still be greater than the original value in order to feed an increased bias to V_2. The magnitude of the error depends on the loop gain, i.e. the gain of V_1 and V_2, and is reduced by increasing the gain as described in Chapter 3.

The performance can be calculated from the equivalent circuit shown in Fig. 5.3, where each valve is represented by an equivalent circuit consisting of a voltage generator $\mu \delta V_g$ having an internal resistance r_a, where μ is the amplification factor and r_a the a.c. resistance of the valve. The current in V_1 and R_1, R_2 will be neglected compared with the load current or

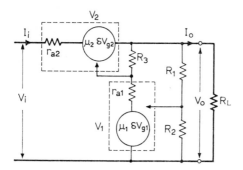

FIG. 5.3 Circuit for calculation of performance of stabilizer

output current I_o. Let the ratio of voltage across R_2 to the output voltage be n; i.e.

$$n = \frac{R_2}{R_1 + R_2}$$

Consider a change of input voltage δV_i which will produce a change of load current δI_o (R_L being constant). Then

$$\delta V_i - \delta I_o r_{a2} + \mu_2 \delta V_{g2} = \delta V_o \qquad (5.1)$$

But $\delta I_o = \delta V_o / R_L$. Substituting in eqn. (5.1),

$$\delta V_i - \frac{\delta V_o r_{a2}}{R_L} + \mu_2 \delta V_{g2} = \delta V_o \qquad (5.2)$$

Considering valve V_1,

$$\delta V_{g1} = n \delta V_o$$

Change of voltage across R_3 which is equal to δV_{g2}

$$= -n \delta V_o \frac{\mu_1 R_3}{R_3 + r_{a1}} \qquad (5.3)$$

This expression neglects the effective resistance across the output terminals, but this makes little difference in practice. The minus sign is required since an increase of voltage across R_3 makes the grid of V_2 more negative. Substituting in eqn. (5.2),

$$\delta V_i - \frac{\delta V_o r_{a2}}{R_L} - n \delta V_o \frac{\mu_1 R_3}{R_3 + r_{a1}} \mu_2 = \delta V_o$$

so that

$$\delta V_i = \delta V_o \left(1 + \frac{r_{a2}}{R_L} + n\mu_1\mu_2 \frac{R_3}{R_3 + r_{a1}}\right)$$

$$= \delta V_o \frac{R_L(R_3 + r_{a1}) + r_{a2}(R_3 + r_{a1}) + R_L n\mu_1\mu_2 R_3}{R_L(R_3 + r_{a1})}$$

$$= \delta V_o \frac{R_3 R_L + R_L r_{a1} + r_{a2} R_3 + r_{a1} r_{a2} + n\mu_1\mu_2 R_3 R_L}{R_L(R_3 + r_{a1})}$$

and the regulation factor is

$$\frac{\delta V_o}{\delta V_i} = \frac{R_L(R_3 + r_{a1})}{R_3 R_L(1 + n\mu_1\mu_2) + R_L r_{a1} + R_3 r_{a2} + r_{a1} r_{a2}}$$

or, since $n\mu_1\mu_2 \gg 1$,

$$\frac{\delta V_o}{\delta V_i} = \frac{R_L(R_3 + r_{a1})}{R_3 R_L n\mu_1\mu_2 + R_L r_{a1} + R_3 r_{a2} + r_{a1} r_{a2}} \qquad (5.4)$$

In most cases the last three terms in the denominator are small compared with the first and can be neglected.

Consider an example:

$$V_o = 200 \text{ V} \qquad I_o = 100 \text{ m A} \qquad \text{Hence } R_L = 2\,\text{k}\Omega$$
$$\mu_1 = 70 \qquad r_{a1} = 50 \text{ k}\Omega$$
$$\mu_2 = 5 \qquad r_{a2} = 1\,\text{k}\Omega$$
$$n = 0\cdot5 \qquad R_3 = 100\,\text{k}\Omega$$

Then

$$\frac{\delta V_o}{\delta V_i} = \frac{2\,(100 + 50)}{(100 \times 2 \times 0\cdot5 \times 70 \times 5) + (2 \times 50) + (100 \times 1) + (50 \times 1)}$$

$$= \frac{300}{35\,000 + 100 + 100 + 50}$$

$$\approx \frac{300}{35\,000} = 0\cdot008\,6$$

Consider a change of load current δI_o, the input voltage V being constant $(\delta V_i = 0)$.

From eqn. (5.1),

$$0 - \delta I_o r_{a2} + \mu_2 \delta V_{g2} = \delta V_o$$

Substituting for δV_{g2} from eqn. (5.3),

$$-\delta I_o r_{a2} - \mu_2 n \delta V_o \frac{\mu_1 R_3}{R_3 + r_{a1}} = \delta V_o$$

or

$$-\delta I_o r_{a2} = \delta V_o \left(1 + \frac{n\mu_1\mu_2 R_3}{R_3 + r_{a1}}\right)$$

$$= \delta V_o \left(\frac{R_3 + r_{a1} + n\mu_1\mu_2 R_3}{R_3 + r_{a1}}\right)$$

and

$$-\frac{\delta V_o}{\delta I_o} = \frac{r_{a2}(R_3 + r_{a1})}{R_3 + r_{a1} + n\mu_1\mu_2 R_3} = R_o \qquad (5.5)$$

where R_o is the output resistance. Normally the first two terms in the denominator will be small compared with the third and can be neglected.

Taking an example and using the same figures as for the calculation of the regulation factor,

$$R_o = \frac{1\,(100 + 50)}{100 + 50 + (0{\cdot}5 \times 70 \times 5 \times 100)} \times 1\,000$$

$$= \frac{150}{100 + 50 + 17\,500} \times 1\,000$$

$$\approx \frac{150}{17\,500} \times 1\,000 = 8{\cdot}6\,\Omega$$

Resistor R_4 may not be necessary, provided that, under all conditions, sufficient current flows in V_1 to maintain the discharge valve under proper operating conditions. Any slope resistance of V_3 tends to reduce the stabilizing action of the circuit. Increase of input voltage causes increased current in R_4 and V_3, and the slope resistance causes an increase of voltage across V_3. Thus the reference voltage increases so increasing the output voltage and reducing the stabilizing action. In a similar way, a rise of output voltage causes an increased current in V_1 and hence in V_3. This again increases the reference voltage and so tends to reduce the stabilizing action.

There are a number of practical difficulties with this circuit. If the grid voltage of V_2 is to be reduced to a low value then the voltage across R_3 must be small. If the loop gain is to be high, R_3 should have as high a value as possible, and hence a small voltage across this resistor can only be obtained by a small current in it and hence in the valve V_1. Operation of a valve at very small currents results in reduced gain as the a.c. resistance increases and the amplification decreases. Thus the upper end of resistor R_3 should go to a point of higher potential than the cathode of V_2. An obvious point is the anode of V_2 as in Fig. 5.4. The disadvantage of this

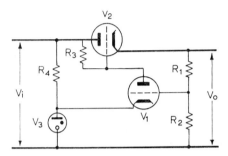

FIG. 5.4 Modified valve stabilizer circuit

arrangement is that the loop gain is now reduced as the upper end of R_3 is no longer taken to a point of fixed voltage. For example, if the input voltage rises, the increase in output voltage results in an increased current in V_1. Not only must this increased current provide a greater negative grid voltage to V_1, but also the increase in input voltage, i.e. the voltage across R_3, is $\delta V_i + \delta V_{g2}$, where δV_{g2} is the voltage fed to V_2. The effect of this change may be an advantage or disadvantage depending on the operating conditions.

When the resistor R_3 is connected to the input,

$$\text{Change of current in } R_3 = \frac{\mu_1 \delta V_{g1} + \delta V_i}{R_3 + r_{a1}}$$

$$\text{Change of voltage across } R_3 = \frac{\mu_1 \delta V_{g1} + \delta V_i}{R_3 + r_{a1}} R_3$$

$$\text{Voltage fed to grid of } V_2 = \delta V_i - \frac{\mu_1 \delta V_{g1} + \delta V_i}{R_3 + r_{a1}} R_3$$

But $\delta V_{g1} = n \delta V_o$. Substituting,

$$\delta V_{g2} = \delta V_i - \frac{\mu_1 n \delta V_o + \delta V_i}{R_3 + r_{a1}} R_3$$

Substituting in eqn. (5.2),

$$\delta V_i - \frac{\delta V_o r_{a2}}{R_L} + \mu_2\left(\delta V_i - \frac{\mu_1 n \delta V_o + \delta V_i}{R_3 + r_{a1}} R_3\right) = \delta V_o$$

$$\delta V_i - \delta V_o \frac{r_{a2}}{R_L} + \mu_2 \delta V_i - \frac{\mu_1 \mu_2 n R_3 \delta V_o}{R_3 + r_{a1}} - \frac{\mu_2 R_3 \delta V_i}{R_3 + r_{a1}} = \delta V_o$$

$$\delta V_i\left(1 - \mu_2 - \frac{\mu_1 R_3}{R_3 + r_{a1}}\right) = \delta V_o\left(1 + \frac{r_{a2}}{R_L} + \frac{\mu_1 \mu_2 n R_3}{R_3 + r_{a1}}\right)$$

$$\delta V_i\left(\frac{R_3 + r_{a1} - \mu_2 R_3 - \mu_2 r_{a1} - \mu_2 R_3}{R_3 + r_{a1}}\right)$$

$$= \delta V_o\left(\frac{R_L R_3 + R_L r_{a1} + R_3 r_{a2} + r_{a1} r_{a2} + \mu_1 \mu_2 n R_3 R_L}{R_L(R_3 + r_{a1})}\right)$$

$$\frac{\delta V_o}{\delta V_i} = \frac{(R_3 + r_{a1} + \mu_1 r_{a1}) R_L}{R_3 R_L n \mu_1 \mu_2 + R_L r_{a1} + R_3 r_{a2} + r_{a1} r_{a2}}$$

$$= \frac{R_L[R_3 + r_{a1}(\mu_2 + 1)]}{R_3 R_L n \mu_1 \mu_2 + R_L r_{a1} + R_3 r_{a2} + r_{a1} r_{a2}} \quad (5.6)$$

This is similar to eqn. (5.4) except that r_{a1} is now replaced by $r_{a1}(\mu_2 + 1)$ in the numerator. This increases the regulation factor and reduces the stability. Using the same figures as in the previous example,

$$\frac{\delta V_o}{\delta V_i} \simeq \frac{2[100 + 50(5 + 1)]}{35\,000} \simeq 0 \cdot 023$$

The changed connection may result in better operating conditions for V_1 so that the a.c. resistance r_{a1} is decreased and the amplification factor μ_1 increased. Thus the overall performance may be better, but this can only be determined in a specific case.

A better arrangement is shown in Fig. 5.5. The valve V_1 is now fed from the voltage across a discharge valve V_4, this being fed with a suitable current through resistor R_5 from the input voltage. Since the voltage across V_4 will be almost constant, the voltage fed to V_1 and R_3 will be almost constant and the current in this circuit need no longer be reduced to a small value in order to obtain a small or zero grid voltage for V_2.

If the output voltage is high then R_1 becomes much larger than R_2, and hence the variation in voltage fed to the grid of V_1 becomes a small fraction of the variation of output voltage. In other words, R_1 and R_2 form an attenuator in front of the amplifier and hence reduce the loop gain and regulation factor. As regards rapid variations of output voltage, such as ripple, the difficulty can be overcome by connecting a capacitor in parallel with R_1. Providing its reactance is low compared with R_2 at the frequencies concerned then the full magnitude of the output voltage variations are fed to V_1 and the performance is improved. The performance under steady conditions may be improved by replacing R_1 by a constant-voltage device such as a discharge valve, so that the variations of output voltage all occur across R_2 and hence are fed to V_1. There are difficulties in this arrangement if it is required to vary the output voltage.

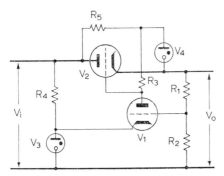

Fig. 5.5 Method of obtaining constant voltage supply for valve V_1

An alternative is to replace R_2 by a constant-current device, i.e. a device with a high slope resistance. Most of the voltage variation will now occur across "R_2". Suitable constant current devices are not readily available, and this arrangement is therefore not commonly used.

Greater gain can be obtained from V_1 if it is a pentode rather than a triode. If the screen grid is fed from the output voltage, i.e. a substantially constant voltage, then the regulation factor is improved by the same amount as the increase in gain due to the use of a pentode. However, by feeding the screen grid from a suitable potential divider across the input as in Fig. 5.6, much better performance can be obtained. (The basic circuit has been shown for feeding V_1, but that of Fig. 5.5 can be used with advantage). Suppose an increase in input voltage occurs. As previously, the grid potential of V_1 moves in a positive direction, increasing the current of V_1, and so increasing the grid–cathode voltage of V_2 and tending to reduce the output voltage. However, part of the increase in input voltage is fed to the screen grid of V_1, and this causes a further increase in anode current. Thus, even if the grid voltage of V_1 did not change, the anode current of V_1 would increase, so increasing the grid–cathode voltage of V_2 and reducing the output voltage. In fact, this circuit operates like a measuring unit across the input and forms an open-loop control system. As was shown in Chapter 3 the regulation factor is

$$R_f = \frac{1 - M_i}{1 + M_o}$$

where M_i is the regulator amplification for the measuring unit across the input, and M_o is the regulator amplification for the measuring unit across the output. Hence if M_i can be made unity the regulation factor becomes

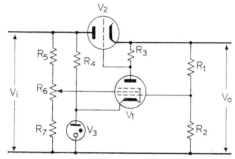

Fig. 5.6 Valve stabilizer circuit using measuring units across input and output

zero. M_i can be varied by varying the setting of R_6 until M_i is approximately unity. If it is not exactly unity then the error is reduced by the factor $1 + M_o$, which is relatively large. In this way a greatly improved performance is possible. For example, suppose M_o is 100; then the regulation factor without this compensation by screen voltage is $1/(100 + 1) = 0 \cdot 009\ 9$. Even if M_i is adjusted so that it is only 0·9 the regulation factor becomes

$$\frac{1 - 0 \cdot 9}{100 + 1} = \frac{0 \cdot 1}{101} = 0 \cdot 000\ 99$$

i.e. an improvement of ten times.

If M_i is less than unity the output voltage will increase with increase of input voltage, but if M_i is made greater than unity an increase in input voltage will result in a decrease in output voltage, i.e. there will be over-compensation. This use of a measuring unit across the input for compensation improves the performance only as regards changes of input voltage (i.e. as regards regulation factor) and does not decrease the output resistance.

The output resistance can be reduced by using a measuring unit effectively in series with the load as described in Chapter 3. One arrangement is shown in Fig. 5.7, where the basic circuit is given, but of course the improvements already mentioned can also be incorporated. A resistor R_5 of low value is now added so that the load current I_L flows through it.

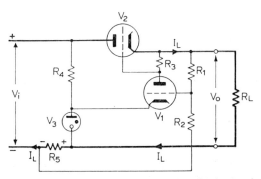

FIG. 5.7 Use of measuring unit in series with load to improve performance

The voltage across R_5 is in the direction shown, and hence as the load current is increased the grid of V_1 is made more negative. This reduces the current of V_1 and hence the grid–cathode voltage of V_2, so reducing its effective resistance and increasing the output voltage. If R_5 is of the correct value this change of grid voltage will just compensate for the normal drop in output voltage (due to the slope resistance of V_2). Again any error is reduced by the factor $1 + M_o$. Over-compensation (i.e. increasing the regulator amplification above unity) will cause the output voltage to rise with increase of load current.

Difficulties arise with these circuits if the output voltage is required to be varied over a wide range. In the basic circuit shown in Fig. 5.2, the output voltage is reduced by decreasing R_1 relative to R_2. However, there is a limit to the minimum voltage at which the circuit will operate. The minimum voltage is equal to the voltage across V_3 plus a reasonable anode voltage for V_1 plus the voltage across R_3 to cut off V_2. Since the minimum voltage for V_3 is about 70 V the minimum output voltage for satisfactory operation is 120–150 V. If voltages less than this are required then an auxiliary negative supply is necessary as in Fig. 5.8. A constant reference voltage is now produced across V_3, and R_1 and R_2 are given values so that, at the correct output voltage, point P is nearly at earth potential (i.e. cathode potential of V_1). Again R_1 and R_2 form an attenuator reducing

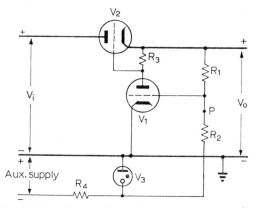

Fig. 5.8 Circuit to enable stabilizer to work to lower output voltages

the loop gain. The output voltage may now be reduced to a value equal to a reasonable anode voltage for V_1 plus the cut-off voltage of V_2.

If the output voltage is to be reduced to a still lower value, the arrangement shown in Fig. 5.9 may be used. With a suitable choice of components the output voltage can then be reduced to zero. Discharge valve V_3 provides a constant cathode voltage for V_1, while V_4 provides a reference voltage against which the output voltage is compared. If a variable voltage

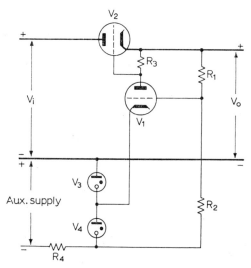

Fig. 5.9 Circuit to enable stabilizer to operate down to zero output voltage

59

is required, R_1 and R_2 are commonly in the form of a variable potential divider. In this diagram only the basic circuit has been shown, but of course the modifications giving improved performance can be incorporated if required.

A large number of variations of the basic circuit are possible, many improving the performance by increasing the loop gain by using a two-stage amplifier in place of V_1, or a cascode amplifier may be used. The power dissipated in V_2 may be large as it is the product of the load current and the difference between the input and output voltages. For a fixed output voltage the difference between the input and output voltages is kept small (i.e. just sufficient for correct operation of V_2) so as to reduce the dissipation of V_2. When the variations of output voltage are large then the dissipation of V_2 increases rapidly. If it is too great for a single valve a number of valves may be used in parallel. In some cases a parallel resistor may be used, but this is suitable only where the load current is approximately constant, since there will be no drop across the resistor with no load current. To reduce the dissipation of V_2 the rectified voltage may be reduced when the output voltage is low. This is done by ganging a switched potential divider (R_1, R_2) to a tapping switch on the transformer secondary feeding the rectifiers.

Pentodes are commonly used for V_2, operated either as triodes (i.e. with screen grid and anode linked) or as pentodes. In the latter case an auxiliary supply is required to feed a constant voltage to the screen grid.

TYPICAL VALUES

The figures will depend on the component values, and the more complex the circuit the better is the performance.

Supply	Fractional stabiliza-tion ratio, S'	Internal resistance	Ripple
		Ω	mV (r.m.s.)
300 V 100 mA: simple circuit	35	5	10
500 V 100 mA: more complex circuit	100	0·5	1
500 V 200 mA: high-precision circuit	5 000	0·02	1

6

Transistor Stabilizer Circuits

Transistor stabilizer circuits follow on the same general lines as valve stabilizer circuits, but circuit design with transistors is more versatile particularly since *p-n-p* and *n-p-n* complementary transistors are available. On the other hand, since transistors are more easily damaged by excess voltage or overload than valves, greater care is necessary in design, and protection circuits are often required. As an open-loop control circuit is not used for the main stabilizer circuit, the measuring unit is always connected across the output. The regulating unit may be connected either in series with the load, or in parallel with it together with a series resistor. The former arrangement is much more common and the power dissipated in the transistor is generally smaller, for a given output power. The disadvantage of the series arrangement is that, if the output terminals are short-circuited, the series transistor carries the short-circuit current and is likely to be burnt out. To prevent this, overload and short-circuit protection circuits are used, and these will be considered later in this chapter.

REGULATING UNIT ACROSS OUTPUT

Circuits with the regulating unit across the output will be considered first. Simple circuits are shown in Fig. 6.1, that at (*a*) using a *p-n-p* transistor and that at (*b*) using an *n-p-n*. One might look upon (*a*) as giving a negative output voltage and upon (*b*) as giving a positive output voltage, but this would be incorrect. Since the input to the stabilizer will be obtained from a rectified transformer voltage, and hence isolated from the mains supply, it is quite unimportant which of the two output terminals is "earthy" and considered as reference. Thus the output from transistorized power supplies is usually isolated from earth and may be used either way round relative to earth (this is also true of some valve stabilizer circuits). For high-precision supplies care may be necessary in design, since there will be capacitance currents flowing in the circuit which cannot be neglected.

In Fig. 6.1 the reference voltage is that of the battery B, and the regulating unit is the transistor TR_1 together with the series resistor R_1. The output voltage will be the battery voltage plus the base–emitter drop of the transistor. Thus, if the input voltage increases, so tending to increase

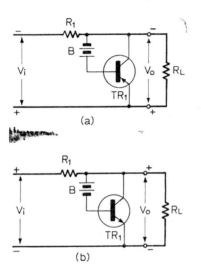

FIG. 6.1 Circuit with regulating unit across output

(*a*) Using *p-n-p* transistor   (*b*) Using *n-p-n* transistor

the output voltage, this will increase the voltage applied to the base relative to the emitter. This results in an increase in collector current and a greater drop in R_1 so tending to compensate for the increase in input voltage. The circuit is extremely simple and has the advantage that no damage is done to the transistor if the output terminals are short-circuited. This results in zero voltage across the transistor and the current is limited by R_1. Since the dissipation in TR_1 tends to be large, the circuit is limited to small power outputs. The resistor R_1 may be placed in the opposite supply lead as in Fig. 6.2 without altering the method of operation or performance.

The battery B is normally replaced by a Zener diode, and simple arrangements are shown in Fig. 6.3, these circuits corresponding to those

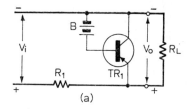

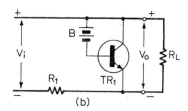

FIG. 6.2 Circuit similar to Fig. 6.1, but with series resistor in opposite lead

(*a*) Using *p-n-p* transistor   (*b*) Using *n-p-n* transistor

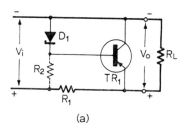

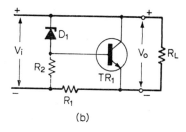

FIG. 6.3 As circuits of Fig. 6.2, but with battery replaced by Zener diode

of Fig. 6.2. Without R_2 the current which flows in the Zener diode D_1 is the base current of transistor TR_1. This is commonly rather small to operate the Zener diode at a suitable point on its characteristic and is also very variable, since it varies with input voltage and load (being approximately proportional to the collector current). Resistor R_2 not only enables the diode to operate at a suitable current, but also reduces the percentage change of current in the diode due to the changing base current of TR_1; but, of course, the current in R_2 and D_1 will vary with change of input voltage, as they are across the input.

The battery in the circuits of Fig. 6.1 also may be replaced by a Zener diode, but in this case a resistor corresponding to R_2 cannot be successfully used. Its corresponding position would be from the base to the emitter of the transistor, and since the base–emitter voltage is a fraction of a volt, it would have to be of very low value and the current would be proportional to the base–emitter voltage of the transistor.

In all these circuits it is important to note that the output voltage is approximately equal to the reference voltage, either that of the battery or the Zener diode. There is no method of altering the output voltage other than by changing the source of reference voltage. A modified circuit which does not have this disadvantage is given in Fig. 6.4. The circuit shown

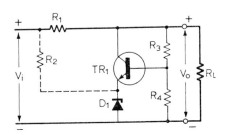

FIG. 6.4 Another circuit with regulating unit across output

uses an *n-p-n* transistor, but an equivalent circuit could be used using a *p-n-p* transistor. If the base–emitter voltage is neglected, then the voltage across R_4 is equal to the voltage across the Zener diode D_1. Since the voltage across R_4 is

$$V_o \frac{R_4}{R_3 + R_4}$$

the output voltage can be varied by varying the ratio of R_3 to R_4. (If large changes are to be made it may also be necessary to alter R_1 or to change the input voltage in order to operate TR_1 under suitable conditions). If the output voltage tends to rise, the base of the transistor is made more positive with respect to the emitter. Hence the collector current increases, so increasing the drop across R_1 and restoring the output to almost its correct value. In this circuit the current in the Zener diode is the emitter current of the transistor, and hence is much larger than in the other circuits and may be sufficient to operate the diode at a suitable point on its characteristic. However, the current will vary as the collector current varies. A resistor R_2 may be added if required to increase the diode current.

Returning to the circuit of Fig. 6.3, the variation of Zener current due to the variation of base current may be reduced by using two transistors in cascade as in Fig. 6.5. This is shown for *n-p-n* transistors, corresponding

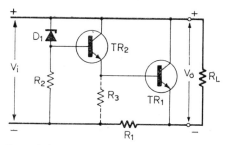

Fig. 6.5 Use of cascade transistors

to Fig. 6.3 (*b*), but of course *p-n-p* transistors may be used with appropriate polarity changes. The base of TR_1 is now supplied from the emitter of TR_2, and hence the base current of TR_2 will be β_2 smaller than the base current of TR_1, where β_2 is the current gain of TR_2. Thus, by using a suitable resistor R_2 to feed the Zener diode, the variations of base current of TR_2 can be quite insignificant. To provide a circuit for the leakage current of TR_1, a resistor R_3 may be added; the purpose of this resistor is considered in more detail later in the chapter. It is not usually of much importance in this circuit, since it is unlikely that TR_1 will be cut off under any normal operating conditions.

The performance of the circuit is dependent on the value of R_1, and like the corresponding discharge-valve or Zener-diode circuit, the performance is improved by increasing the value of R_1. If the current is to

65

remain the same then the input voltage V_i must be increased, so reducing the efficiency of the circuit. An improvement can be made by replacing R_1 by a constant-current device, i.e. a device with a low d.c. resistance but high slope resistance. One possible arrangement is given in Fig. 6.6, the

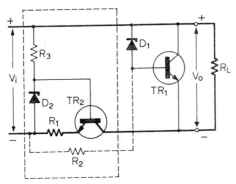

Fig. 6.6 Replacement of series resistor by constant-current circuit

portion shown in the dotted rectangle being the constant-current circuit. This is equivalent to Fig. 6.3 (*b*) with the resistor R_1 replaced by the constant-current circuit. An equivalent circuit using *p-n-p* transistors may be constructed. The Zener diode D_2 is fed through R_3 and hence maintains the base of TR_2 at a constant voltage relative to the negative input terminal. The voltage across R_1 must therefore be this constant voltage minus the base–emitter drop of TR_2. Since the latter is small and almost constant, the drop across R_1 is nearly constant and hence a constant current must flow through it. This current is the emitter current and also the collector current (neglecting the base current) of TR_2. Thus the circuit acts as a constant-current device having a relatively low d.c. resistance. The circuits shown have not a good performance since there is little gain between the measuring unit and the regulating unit. The performance can be improved by connecting an amplifier between the Zener diode and the regulating unit, transistor TR_1.

REGULATING UNIT IN SERIES WITH LOAD

Circuits where the regulating unit is in series with the load will now be considered. The simplest arrangement is given in Fig. 6.7, where the battery B provides the reference voltage of the measuring unit and TR_1

forms the regulating unit. If the output voltage tends to rise it reduces the base–emitter voltage and hence tends to cut off TR_1, so reducing the output voltage to an equilibrium value. This circuit is, in fact, a common-collector or emitter-follower circuit in which the reference voltage V_R from the battery is the input and, of course, V_o is the output. To a first approximation the gain of such an amplifier is unity, and hence, if the battery voltage is constant, the output voltage V_o is constant.

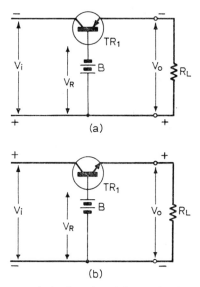

FIG. 6.7 Simple emitter-follower circuit

(*a*) Using *p-n-p* transistor   (*b*) Using *n-p-n* transistor

If the base–emitter voltage is small compared with the reference voltage V_R the performance is quite good. For example, with a particular transistor, changing the collector current from 1 to 10 A only requires a change of base–emitter voltage from 300 to 450 mV, or 150 mV. At low currents the change is rather greater, being 300 mV from 0 to 1 A. Provided that this change is small compared with the output voltage, reasonable regulation and regulation factor result. There is, of course, an equivalent valve circuit (cathode follower), but this is of little value for this purpose, because the grid–cathode voltage change for, say, a 10:1 change of anode current is large, say 10 V, and cannot therefore be small compared with the output voltage unless the latter is several thousand volts.

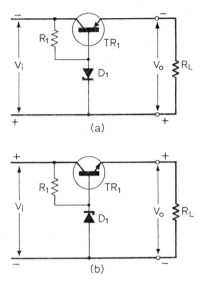

FIG. 6.8 Emitter-follower circuit using Zener diode for reference voltage

(*a*) Using *p-n-p* transistor   (*b*) Using *n-p-n* transistor

The battery B shown in Fig. 6.7 is normally replaced by a Zener diode as shown in Fig. 6.8, where the Zener diode D_1 is fed with a suitable current through resistor R_1 from the input voltage (it cannot be fed from the output voltage since this is slightly less than the base voltage). If the voltage across D_1 is constant, any change of output voltage is due to the change of base–emitter voltage. It is interesting to compare germanium and silicon transistors. Some results obtained by the author are given in Table 6.1.

TABLE 6.1

	Germanium OC36	Silicon 2N3715
	V	V
Base–emitter drop at 10 mA	0·13	0·58
Base–emitter drop at 1 A	0·40	0·86
Change of base–emitter drop	0·27	0·28

A minimum current of 10 mA was used, as at currents less than this misleading results are easily obtained due to leakage currents and instrument currents. As would be expected, the actual drop across the silicon transistor is considerably greater, but the *change* of base–emitter drop from 10 mA to 1 A is almost the same. It is the latter figure which is important when considering the regulation of the circuit. The actual figures will depend on the actual transistors used, but those in the table appear to be typical.

Unfortunately, the voltage across the Zener diode is not constant because the current in it changes and it has a finite slope resistance. The Zener current changes because the input voltage and the base current of the transistor change. If it is assumed that the emitter-follower circuit is fed from a rectified supply (as is normal), then changes in mains supply will, of course, result in proportional changes of the input voltage V_i. The effect of load is more complicated. If the load current increases there will be a greater base–emitter drop as already discussed, but there will also be an increase in base current, this being equal to the product of $1/\beta$ and the change of load current. The directions of the various currents are shown in Fig. 6.9, where it is seen that $I_R = I_b + I_d$. Since the current in

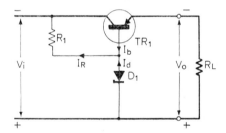

FIG. 6.9 Directions of currents in emitter-follower circuit

R_1 is approximately constant, if I_b increases then I_d must decrease by the same amount. The input voltage V_i will also decrease with an increase in load current by an amount determined by the regulation of the rectifier circuit. This is by no means small, and the change is likely to be of the same order as that due to changes of mains voltages from 210 to 250 V. Thus, when the load changes the input voltage changes, resulting in a change of current in R_1, the Zener current changes owing to change of base current, and there is a change of base–emitter drop.

The change of input voltage V_i will first be considered as regards its effect on the current in the Zener diode. This voltage changes, as has been shown, owing to changes of supply voltage and of load. A given percentage change of input voltage V_i can cause a much greater percentage change of current in R_1 and the Zener diode D_1, since the voltage across R_1 is the difference between V_i and the approximate constant voltage across D_1. For example, suppose that the nominal voltage across the Zener diode is 23 V and R_1 is 350 Ω. Using a 25–0–25 V transformer and silicon rectifiers, the rectified voltage in a typical case changed as in Table 6.2.

TABLE 6.2

Mains voltage, V_m	Load current, I_L	Rectified voltage, V_i
V		V
230	10 mA	34·7
230	1 A	29·4
250	10 mA	37·7
210	1 A	26·9

Thus at 230 V and 10 mA load current, the voltage across R_1 is $34·7 - 23 = 11·7$ V, and hence the current in R_1 is 33·4 mA. At 230 V and 1 A the voltage is $29·4 - 23 = 6·4$ V and the current is 18·3 mA. Hence the change of current in the Zener diode is $33·4 - 18·3 = 15·1$ mA if the base current of the transistor is neglected. If the Zener diode has a slope resistance of 35 Ω (a typical figure) then the change of voltage is $15·1 \times 35 \times 10^{-3} = 0·53$ V, which is almost ~~as~~ TWICE great as that due to the change of base–emitter voltage given in Table 6.1. The change of current in R_1 and D_1 can be reduced by

(a) Increasing the value of R_1, but, in order to maintain the same current, the voltage V_i must be increased. This has the disadvantage of increasing the drop across the transistor and hence increasing its dissipation and decreasing the efficiency of the circuit.

(b) Using two Zener diodes in cascade. This is difficult unless there is a reasonable difference between input and output voltages.

(c) Feeding R_1 from a separate supply of either the same or preferably a higher voltage. Changes of mains voltage will, of course, cause corresponding changes in this voltage, but changes of load current will not alter it, and hence an improved performance is obtained as regards load changes. Performance is improved still further if cascade Zener diodes are used, this being quite practical as the separate supply can be made of suitable voltage to operate the circuit.

(*d*) Replacing R_1 by a constant-current circuit.

A possible arrangement is shown in Fig. 6.10, where R_1, D_2, TR_2 and R_2 form the constant-current circuit. The Zener diode D_2 is fed with a suitable current through R_2. The voltage across R_1 is equal to that across

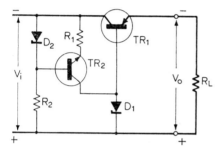

FIG. 6.10 Use of constant-current circuit to feed Zener diode

D_2 (constant) less the base–emitter drop of TR_2. The latter can be made small compared with the drop across D_2, and hence the voltage across R_1 is almost constant. This means a constant current in R_1 and TR_2, and hence in D_1. This greatly improves the performance. In a typical case the change was reduced from 0·86 (using a series resistor) to 0·17 (using the constant-current circuit) for a mains voltage change from 210–250 V. For changes of load current from 10 mA to 1 A it was reduced from 1·19 to 0·73 V.

Turning now to the change of base current of the main transistor, which causes a corresponding change of current in the Zener diode, let the current gain of the transistor be 90. For a change of load current from 10 mA to 1 A the change of base current is $(1\,000 - 10)/90 = 11$ mA.

The change of current in the Zener diode due to this change of base current will be approximately the same, and assuming a Zener diode slope resistance of 35 Ω, the change of voltage will be $11 \times 35 \times 10^{-3} = 0·38$ V. This is greater than the change of base–emitter voltage.

From earlier figures, for a load current of 10mA the current in R_1 was 33·4 mA, and at a load current of 1 A it was 18·3mA. Allowing now for the change of base current, for a load of 10 mA the current in the Zener diode is 33·4 mA (since the base current is negligible), while for a load current of 1 A it is $18·3 - 11 = 7·3$ mA. Thus the total change of current in the Zener diode is $33·4 - 7·3 = 26·1$ mA. Using the slope resistance of 35 Ω this gives a voltage change of $26·1 \times 35 \times 10^{-3} = 0·913$ V. It is therefore seen that the performance of the circuit is poor, mainly because the Zener diode voltage changes rather than owing to the performance of the emitter follower itself. Obviously the variation of base current cannot be changed, but its effect on the Zener diode can be made much smaller by connecting a current amplifier between the main transistor TR_1 and the Zener diode D_1.

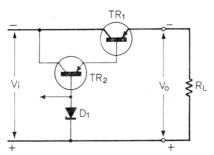

FIG. 6.11 Use of compound emitter-follower, Darlington pair or super-alpha pair

One basic arrangement is shown in Fig. 6.11, where TR_1 is the main transistor and TR_2 the current amplifier. The circuit is known under such names as *compound emitter-follower, Darlington pair* and *super-alpha pair*. It is an important circuit as it is used in many stabilizer circuits other than emitter-follower circuits. The base current of TR_2 is now the product of the load current and $1/\beta_1\beta_2$, where β_1 and β_2 are the current gains of TR_1 and TR_2 respectively. In this way the effect of the base current on D_1 may be reduced by, say, a factor of 100 and often becomes negligible.

The problem of the leakage current of TR_1 must now be considered, and this is illustrated in Fig. 6.12. The directions of the currents due to the load current in the emitter and base leads are shown. The collector leakage current flows from base to collector (for *p-n-p*) as shown. Thus the actual current in the base lead of TR_1 is the difference between the normal base current due to load and the leakage current. When the base

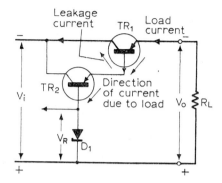

FIG. 6.12 Leakage current of main transistor

current due to the load becomes smaller than the leakage current, the base current tends to reverse. However, this reverse current cannot flow in TR_2, and hence the base of TR_1 is effectively open-circuited and TR_2 no longer has any control over TR_1. To prevent this a resistor R_1 may be added as in Fig. 6.13. Provided that the current I_R in resistor R_1 is greater

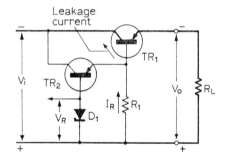

FIG. 6.13 Use of resistor R_1 to overcome effect of leakage current

than the leakage current of TR_1, TR_2 will be able to control the base current of TR_1 and hence the output. The difference between I_R and the leakage current flows in the emitter circuit of TR_2, and hence I_R should not be greater than necessary.

It will be seen from Fig. 6.13 that the output voltage will be the reference voltage across D_1 less the base–emitter drops of TR_1 and TR_2. Thus, by using the amplifier circuit, two base–emitter drops have now been included between the reference voltage and the output. However, the drop across

TR$_2$ is normally small and does not vary much, because the current is much smaller than the load current. By using this amplifier circuit the change of current in the Zener diode due to load changes becomes small and often negligible. For example, if the load current is 1 A and the current gains are $\beta_1 = 40$ $\beta_2 = 50$, then the base current of TR$_2$ is $1\,000/(40 \times 50) = 0\cdot5$ mA. This can be made small compared with the normal current in D$_1$.

An alternative compound emitter-follower circuit using complementary transistors is shown in Fig. 6.14. The main transistor, TR$_1$, is now fed

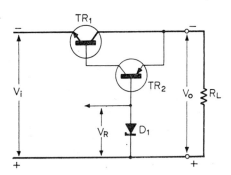

FIG. 6.14 Compound emitter-follower circuit using complementary transistors

from the collector of TR$_2$. This circuit has the advantage that there is only one base–emitter drop between the reference voltage across D$_1$ and the output. This is the drop across TR$_2$, which is carrying only a small current. In typical circuits (using a constant-current circuit to feed the Zener diode) the changes of output voltage for load changes of 10 mA to 1 A are given in Table 6.3.

TABLE 6.3

	Change of output voltage
	V
Single transistor	0·28
Compound transistors	0·36
Compound transistors using complementary pair	0·09

It will be seen that the performance of the complementary-pair circuit is far superior.

It is possible to compensate for the voltage drop in the series transistor and details are given in Ref. 10.

It is important to consider the problem of ripple. There will, of course, be some ripple in the output voltage from the rectifier, and it is desirable that this be reduced to as small a value as possible. Provided that the reference voltage has no ripple, little ripple will appear in the output since the circuit acts as a voltage stabilizer to input voltage changes. Looking at it another way, variations of collector voltage cause little change of collector current, owing to the characteristics of the transistor. However, there will be some ripple on the reference voltage if a Zener diode is used, since it is fed from the input voltage. If the ripple voltage across the input is V_{rip} volts, the ripple voltage across the Zener diode will be

$$\frac{R_z}{R_z + R_1} \, V_{rip} \text{ (neglecting the effect of base current)}$$

where R_z is the a.c. slope resistance of the Zener diode, and R_1 is the resistance feeding the diode.

Considering an example where R_1 is $350\,\Omega$ and R_z is $10\,\Omega$ (the a.c. slope resistance will be lower than the d.c. slope resistance, which has been used in the earlier calculations), the ripple is

$$\frac{10}{350 + 10} \, V_{rip} = 0 \cdot 028 \, V_{rip}$$

This will be approximately the ripple on the output voltage and is much less than the ripple across the output of the rectifier. The ripple on the rectified voltage can be reduced by increasing the value of the reservoir capacitor, but this method is expensive and takes up considerable space. It is much better to reduce the ripple by connecting a suitable capacitor across the Zener diode. If the reactance of the capacitor is small compared with R_z and R_1 then the ripple across the Zener diode becomes

$$\frac{X_c}{R_1} \, V_{rip}$$

where X_c is the reactance of the capacitor.

Consider an example where the capacitor has a value of $900\,\mu\mathrm{F}$ and $R_1 = 350\,\Omega$, X_c will be $1\cdot8\,\Omega$ (assuming $100\,\mathrm{Hz}$ ripple). The ripple across the Zener diode will now be

$$\frac{1\cdot8}{350}\,V_{rip} = 0\cdot0051\,V_{rip}$$

and this will be approximately that across the output. The capacitor is much more effective in this position than across the reservoir capacitor. If a constant-current circuit is used then R_1 becomes the slope resistance of the circuit, which is high. Thus a constant-current circuit gives greatly reduced ripple across the output of the stabilizer compared with the use of a resistor feeding the Zener diode.

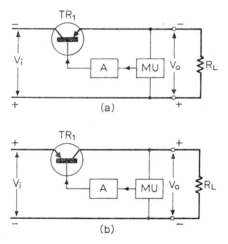

FIG. 6.15 Use of amplifier between measuring unit and regulating unit

The performance of emitter-follower circuits is limited as there is no amplification between the measuring and regulating units. Improved performance can be obtained by the use of a voltage amplifier between the measuring and regulating units, and two circuits are shown in Fig. 6.15. In both cases *p-n-p* transistors are shown, but, as before, equivalent circuits using *n-p-n* transistors are possible. Circuit (*a*) may be considered as an emitter follower with the addition of an amplifier, whereas in circuit (*b*) the output is taken from the collector. An example of circuit (*a*) is given in Fig. 6.16. Resistors R_1 and R_2 form a potential divider across the output, and in transistor TR_2 the voltage across R_2 is compared with the reference voltage across Zener diode D_1. Thus, if the output voltage rises, the base of TR_2 goes more negative and the collector current of TR_2 increases. This increases the voltage drop across R_3 and hence the

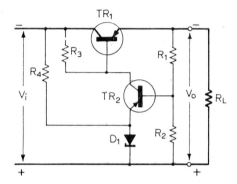

FIG. 6.16 Circuit with amplifier between measuring and regulating units

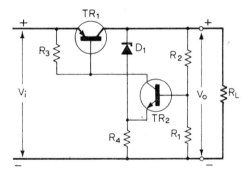

FIG. 6.17 Another circuit with amplifier between measuring and regulating units

base voltage of TR_1 falls. Since TR_1 is connected as an emitter follower, the emitter voltage and output fall, so tending to restore the output voltage to its correct value. Resistor R_4 is used to maintain a suitable current in the Zener diode.

An example of the basic circuit of Fig. 6.15 (*b*) is shown in Fig. 6.17. Again R_1 and R_2 form a potential divider across the output terminals and the voltage across R_2 is compared with that across the Zener diode D_1

by the transistor TR_2. If the output voltage rises then the voltage across R_2 increases, so making the base more negative with respect to its emitter. Since this is an *n-p-n* transistor, the collector current is reduced, resulting in reduced voltage across resistor R_3. This results in reduced base–emitter voltage of TR_1, so increasing its effective resistance and reducing the output voltage.

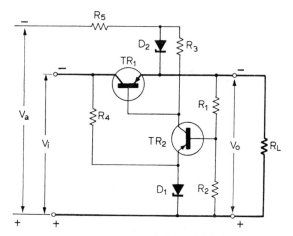

FIG. 6.18 Use of circuit to supply constant voltage to transistor TR_2

In both these circuits the loop gain and hence performance are reduced by the use of a potential divider, but the potential divider allows the output voltage to be varied. Improvement is possible by replacing resistor R_1 by a constant-voltage device (e.g. a Zener diode) so that the actual change of output voltage is fed to TR_2 rather than a fraction of it. The disadvantage of the arrangement is that the output voltage is fixed, being approximately the sum of the two Zener diode voltages. In Fig. 6.16 the resistor R_3 is returned to the input voltage (a varying voltage), which means that, if the input voltage rises (so increasing the output voltage), the voltage across R_3 must rise to make up for the increase in input voltage. This effectively reduces the loop gain. The same problem arose in the equivalent valve circuit. The resistor R_3 cannot be connected to the output (i.e. emitter of TR_1) as this is at a lower voltage than the base.

An improvement is obtained by feeding R_3 from a constant voltage as in Fig. 6.18. The Zener diode D_2 is fed from an auxiliary supply V_a, through resistor R_5. Thus the upper end of D_2 is at an approximately constant voltage and the effective loop gain is increased. If the input voltage is high enough, V_a may be dispensed with and D_2 fed off the input voltage. However, increasing V_i increases the dissipation in TR_1 and reduces the efficiency of the circuit.

The collector current of TR_2 is approximately the base current of TR_1 (in both Figs. 6.16 and 6.17). When the load current is large this current becomes excessive for TR_2 (the current may be excessive for D_1 and the base current of TR_2 may begin to load the potential divider R_1, R_2), and a current amplifier is required between TR_2 and TR_1. This normally takes the form of the compound emitter-follower for the circuit of Fig. 6.16 and already considered in Figs. 6.11, 6.12 and 6.13. Similar (not complementary) transistors are generally used, as the additional base–emitter drop is not now important. A compound circuit using three transistors may also be used. In Fig. 6.17 the current amplifier would generally be a common emitter.

There is obviously an almost unlimited range of circuits that can be used, but all depend on the same general principles. The performance is improved by (*a*) having a very stable reference-voltage source, and (*b*) increasing the loop gain. The stable reference-voltage source is produced by feeding the reference diode off a constant-current circuit or using a pre-stabilizer to feed the Zener diode circuit, and using a Zener diode which has been selected for its long-term stability and low temperature coefficient (or used in a suitable temperature compensating circuit). In some cases the Zener diode may be placed in a constant-temperature oven.

As well as using a large loop gain, it is important that no drift should occur in the amplifier, and it is common practice to use a long-tailed pair, or differential amplifier, as in Fig. 6.19. The reference voltage is fed between A and B and the stabilizer output voltage or a fraction of it is fed to C and D. If TR_1 and TR_2 are matched, or are a twin transistor, the effect of temperature is greatly reduced, particularly if the output voltage is taken between points X and Y.

A useful basic stabilizer circuit is shown in Fig. 6.20, which is commonly used and has some advantages. The reference voltage is V_R (shown as a battery voltage for convenience), which, together with the output voltage V_o feeds the potential divider R_1, R_2. The difference in voltage between P and Q is amplified in the amplifier A and fed to the regulating-unit transistor TR_1. Provided that the gain of the amplifier is large, the voltage between P and Q must always be small and can be assumed zero. Hence

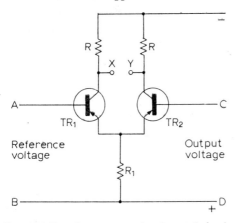

FIG. 6.19 Transistors arranged as long-tailed pair

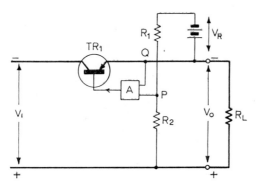

FIG. 6.20 Basic stabilizer circuit

the voltage across R_2 must equal the output voltage V_o, and that across R_1 must equal the reference voltage V_R. Thus

$$\frac{V_o}{V_R} = \frac{V_{R_2}}{V_{R_1}}$$

but the same current flows in R_1 and R_2 (neglecting any current into the amplifier), and hence the voltages across the resistors are proportional to the resistances. Hence

$$\frac{V_o}{V_R} = \frac{R_2}{R_1} \quad \text{or} \quad V_o = V_R \frac{R_2}{R_1}$$

Thus the output voltage V_o is proportional to R_2. The output voltage can therefore be made variable by making R_2 variable. Because of the proportionality the stabilizer can be easily programmed by using suitable resistors. This will be reconsidered later. Also the output voltage is inversely proportional to R_1, but this feature is less useful.

The circuit can be modified to that of Fig. 6.21. As before, the voltage across P and Q may be taken as zero, and hence the same relationship can be calculated. However, the circuit can be redrawn to look like an amplifier

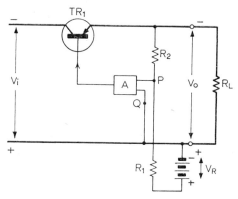

FIG. 6.21 Alternative basic stabilizer circuit

circuit as in Fig. 6.22. The circuit now becomes that of an operational amplifier with feedback by means of R_2. Using the virtual earth idea (i.e. P and Q at the same potential), the gain of the circuit is R_2/R_1. The input to the amplifier is V_R, and hence the output voltage is $V_R (R_2/R_1)$, the same relationship as previously calculated. Provided that V_R is constant, the output voltage is constant. In fact a device is manufactured which can be used either as an amplifier or as a stabilizer.

As in valve stabilizers, measuring units may be connected across the input and in series with the load to improve the performance. A circuit with this feature together with some others already considered is shown in Fig. 6.23. Leaving out the effect of R_5 and R_9, the output voltage feeds the potential divider R_1, R_2, R_7, and the voltage across R_2, R_7 is compared with the reference voltage across the Zener diode D_1. Any difference is amplified in TR_3 with its load resistor R_3 fed from the constant voltage across D_2. TR_1 and TR_2 form a Darlington pair and only a small current has to be fed to the base of TR_2 from TR_3.

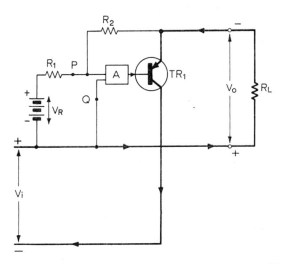

FIG. 6.22 Circuit of Fig. 6.21 drawn as operational amplifier

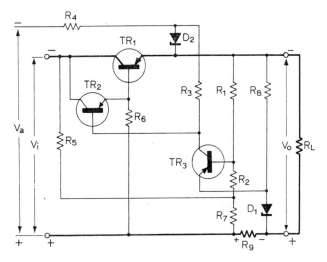

FIG. 6.23 Complete transistor stabilizer circuit

First consider the effect of R_5. If the input voltage rises, additional current will flow in R_5 and hence the voltage across R_7 will be increased. This causes the base potential of TR_3 to rise (in a negative direction) so increasing the collector current of TR_3. This in turn causes an increased drop across R_3, so reducing the base voltages of TR_2 and TR_1 and reducing the output voltage. This therefore compensates for change of input voltage if the resistor values are correctly chosen.

The effect of R_9 will now be considered. If the load current increases then the voltage across R_9 increases in the direction shown, making the emitter of TR_3 more negative (since the voltage across D_1 is constant). This reduces the collector current of TR_3, so decreasing the drop across R_3. Thus the base voltages of TR_2 and TR_1 rise, so tending to increase the output voltage to make up for the drop due to increased load current. If R_9 is of the correct value good compensation is possible, with a resultant decrease in output resistance. In both cases any error in compensation is reduced by the action of the measuring unit across the output. Using this idea greatly improved performance is possible.

TRANSISTOR DISSIPATION

The dissipation of the series transistor is important and should normally be kept to a minimum. A case of a stabilizer with a fixed output voltage will be considered first. The input voltage should obviously be no greater than necessary, since the dissipation in the transistor is the product of load current and the difference between the input and output voltages. Under the worst operating conditions the voltage across the series transistor must not fall below, say, 1 or 2 V. The worst conditions will be maximum load and minimum input voltage, but allowance must be made for the ripple voltage from the rectifiers, as at no part of the cycle must the voltage drop across the transistor be less than the above figure. It might be supposed that maximum dissipation will occur at full load, but this is not always the case because the rectifier voltage (i.e. input voltage to the stabilizer circuit) depends on the load current.

Thus suppose the rectified voltage (input voltage to stabilizer) is given by

$$V_{NL} - IR_i$$

83

where V_{NL} is the no-load voltage and R_i is the effective internal resistance. If the output voltage is V_o then the voltage across the series transistor is

$$V_{NL} - IR_i - V_o$$

and the dissipation is given by

$$P = (V_{NL} - IR_i - V_o)I = IV_{NL} - I^2 R_i - IV_o \tag{6.1}$$

The current for maximum dissipation is obtained by differentiating with respect to I and equating to zero:

$$V_{NL} - 2IR_i - V_o = 0$$

or

$$I = \frac{V_{NL} - V_o}{2R_i} \tag{6.2}$$

Suppose that $V_{NL} = 40\,\text{V}$, $V_o = 30\,\text{V}$ and $R_i = 5\,\Omega$. Then maximum dissipation occurs when

$$I = \frac{40 - 30}{2 \times 5} = 1\,\text{A}$$

and from eqn. (6.1) the dissipation is

$$40 - 5 - 30 = 5\,\text{W}$$

If the full-load current is $1 \cdot 5\,\text{A}$ then the dissipation at full load is

$$(40 \times 1\cdot5) - (2\cdot25 \times 5) - (1\cdot5 \times 30) = 3\cdot8\,\text{W}$$

The manner in which the dissipation varies between no load and full load will depend on the regulation of the rectifier circuit and on the relationship between input and output voltages, but it is seen that maximum dissipation does not necessarily occur at full load.

For satisfactory operation the transistor must satisfy a number of conditions:

(*a*) The maximum rated collector–emitter voltage must not be exceeded. The voltage across the transistor will be a maximum under no load and with maximum mains voltage. The transistor rating should be rather greater than this to allow for surges, etc.

(*b*) The maximum rated collector current must not be exceeded. This is, of course, the maximum load current plus any current taken by potential dividers or bleed resistors.

(*c*) The maximum rated collector dissipation must not be exceeded. This has already been calculated. The transistor must be able to dissipate this power under the condition of maximum temperature, and allowance must be made for the maximum ambient temperature within the case of the stabilizer.

(*d*) The combination of collector current and voltage must not bring the operating point within the secondary breakdown area of the transistor, shown shaded in Fig. 6.24. If the transistor is operated

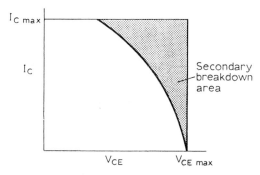

FIG. 6.24 Diagram showing secondary breakdown area

in this area it is likely to suffer failure by secondary breakdown [12] due to local overheating. A check must therefore be made to see that the operating point never goes into this region. The limits of the area are specified by the transistor manufacturers.

Much more severe operating conditions may occur with overload or short-circuit of the output terminals of the stabilizer; these conditions will be considered later.

There is an obvious limit to the power that can be dissipated by a single transistor even on a large heat sink, and hence methods will now be considered of increasing the possible dissipation by, for example, the use of more than one transistor.

TRANSISTORS IN PARALLEL

One obvious method is to use transistors in parallel as in Fig. 6.25 (*a*). Provided that the dissipation is shared equally by the transistors then the total permitted regulation-unit power will be *n* times the maximum

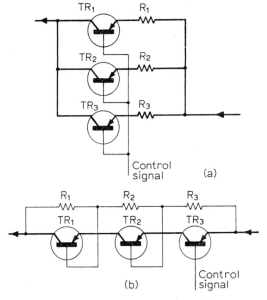

FIG. 6.25 Transistors in parallel and in series
(*a*) Parallel   (*b*) Series

dissipation of one transistor, where n is the number of transistors in parallel. Unfortunately the variation of base–emitter drop between transistors is large and load sharing is not good. Load sharing can be improved by using emitter resistors R_1, R_2, R_3 as shown. However, to get close load sharing the power dissipated in these resistors becomes large (see Ref. 11), and hence some compromise must be made between ideal load sharing and excessive dissipation in the resistors. Therefore it is normally necessary to derate the transistors to prevent overloading.

TRANSISTORS IN SERIES

An alternative method of spreading the dissipation among a number of transistors is to connect them in series. However, some method of ensuring that they share the total voltage equally must be used. One method is shown in Fig. 6.25 (*b*).

Three equal-value resistors R_1, R_2, R_3 are used. Thus the voltage between the base of TR_2 and the emitter of TR_3 must be one-third of the total. The voltage between the base of TR_1 and the base of TR_2 must be one-third, and that between the collector of TR_1 and its base must also be one-third. Since the base–emitter drop is small, the collector–emitter voltages of the transistors are equal for practical purposes. This arrangement has limited use, since it does not increase the current rating but only the voltage rating; it is mainly of use in relatively high-voltage stabilizers.

Another way of sharing the dissipation (not necessarily equally) is shown in Fig. 6.26. With the figures shown, the collector–base voltage

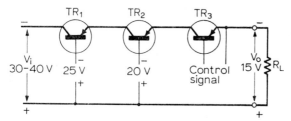

FIG. 6.26 Transistors as prestabilizers

(near enough, the collector–emitter voltage) of TR_1 will be 5–15 V. That of TR_2 will be 5 V and that of TR_3 approximately 5 V. The actual dissipations can be varied by varying the fixed voltage applied to the bases of TR_1 and TR_2. This circuit has the advantage that TR_1 and TR_2 act as simple stabilizers (actually emitter followers) in front of the main controlled transistor TR_3. Thus the variations of voltage across TR_3 are reduced to a small amount and the performance is improved. In other words, TR_1 and TR_2 act as pre-stabilizers or pre-regulators, reducing the variations of input voltage to the main stabilizer.

TRANSISTOR IN PARALLEL WITH A RESISTOR

The power dissipation in a transistor can be reduced by the use of a parallel resistor, R_1, as in Fig. 6.27. If the transistor is cut off then all the current

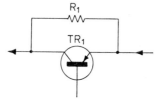

FIG. 6.27 Resistor in parallel with transistor

flows in the resistor and all the power is dissipated in it. When the transistor is fully conducting (i.e. bottomed) the voltage drop across it will be small and hence practically all the current will flow in the transistor. Since the drop across the transistor is small the power dissipated in it also is small. If the transistor is considered as equivalent to a variable resistor then the circuit can be redrawn as in Fig. 6.28, where R_2 represents the

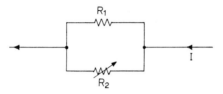

Fig. 6.28 Fixed and variable resistors in parallel—equivalent circuit of Fig. 6.27

transistor. When the transistor is cut off, R_2 is infinite, and when it is fully conducting, R_2 will be assumed to be of zero resistance. Let the load current, I, be constant.

$$\text{Voltage across regulating unit, } V_R = I\frac{R_1 R_2}{R_1 + R_2}$$

$$\text{Dissipation in } R_2, (P_{R2}), = \frac{V_R^2}{R_2} = \left(\frac{IR_1 R_2}{R_1 + R_2}\right)^2 \frac{1}{R_2} \tag{6.3}$$

The dissipation is a maximum when $dP_{R2}/dR_2 = 0$. Differentiating eqn. (6.3) and equating to zero gives $R_1 = R_2$. Thus maximum dissipation occurs in the variable resistor R_2 when it has a value equal to R_1.

Substituting this condition in eqn. (6.3), the maximum dissipation in R_2 is

$$\left(\frac{IR_1^2}{2R_1}\right)^2 \frac{1}{R_1} = \frac{I^2 R_1}{4}$$

The maximum dissipation in the regulating unit occurs when R_2 is infinite, and is then $I^2 R_1$. Thus the maximum dissipation in the variable element R_2 is one-quarter of the maximum dissipation of the regulating unit and occurs when $R_1 = R_2$. The maximum dissipation in R_1 is, of course, $I^2 R_1$, the maximum dissipation of the regulating unit.

In this way, for a given regulating unit dissipation, the transistor dissipation is decreased. However, the current that the transistor must carry is I, i.e. twice the value when the dissipation is a maximum. Also the maximum transistor voltage is the maximum which occurs across the regulating unit and again twice the value at maximum dissipation.

As before, it is important to make certain that the transistor does not operate in the secondary breakdown area. The operation is shown graphically in Fig. 6.29. The line R_1 is drawn with a slope of $- 1/R_1$ from

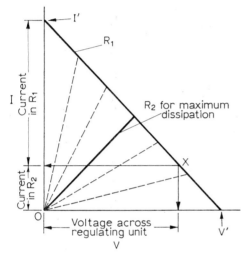

Fig. 6.29 Operation of fixed and variable resistors in parallel

the point V' corresponding to maximum regulating unit voltage. The line R_2 is drawn from the origin and varies in slope, $1/R_2$, as R_2 changes from zero to infinity. When R_2 has the same slope as R_1 the dissipation in R_2 is a maximum. The manner in which the currents are shared and the voltage across the regulating unit are shown for a typical operating point X.

The use of a resistor in this way has the serious disadvantage that the maximum drop across the regulating unit is proportional to the load current and is zero at zero current. This arrangement is only suitable for a stabilizer with a load current which is approximately constant.

The difficulty may be overcome by the use of two transistors and one fixed resistor. The circuit operates on the principle of using a transistor and resistor in parallel for large currents and low voltages, and a transistor and resistor in series for small currents and large voltages. The basic principle is shown in Fig. 6.30, where the two transistors are represented

89

by variable resistors R_2, R_3. For large currents, R_3 is made zero and R_2 is varied so that we now have a fixed and variable resistor in parallel, as already described, with the advantage that the maximum dissipation in R_2 is a quarter of the maximum regulating unit dissipation. For small currents R_2 is made infinite and R_3 varied; thus R_1 and R_3 are in series.

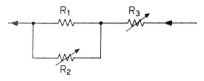

Fig. 6.30 Method of overcoming disadvantage of resistor and transistor in parallel

If one considers that the voltage drop, V, across the regulating unit is constant and the current is variable then the power dissipated in R_3 is given by

$$I^2 R_3 = \left(\frac{V}{R_1 + R_3} \right)^2 R_3$$

In a similar way to the previous case, if this expression is differentiated with respect to R_3 and equated to zero, then the condition $R_1 = R_3$ results for maximum dissipation in R_3. Also, the dissipation in R_3 is a quarter of the maximum occurring in the regulating unit, consisting of R_1 and R_3 in series.

It is useful to consider some actual figures. Let the regulating unit carry a maximum current of 1 A with a maximum voltage drop of 10 V. The value of R_1 ($R_2 = \infty$ and $R_3 = 0$) must be 10/1, or 10 Ω. The maximum dissipation in the regulating unit is therefore $I^2 \times 10 = 10$ W. Figures for various conditions are shown in Table 6.4.

In the first portion of the table the voltage across the regulating unit is taken as the maximum value, and this is maintained at currents less than 1 A by varying R_3. It will be noted that maximum dissipation occurs at half maximum current. In the second portion of the table the current has been taken as constant at the maximum value and the drop across the regulating unit varied. As the drop across R_1 alone would be excessive, R_2 is used to reduce it, and thus maximum dissipation occurs at half maximum voltage. In both cases the maximum dissipation is 2·5 W, one-quarter of the maximum regulating-unit dissipation, which agrees with

TABLE 6.4

Current	Voltage across regulating unit	Voltage across R_1 and R_2	Value of R_2	Dissipation in R_2	Voltage across R_3	Value of R_3	Dissipation in R_3
A	V	V	∞	W	V	Ω	W
1	10	10	∞	0	0	0	0
0·9	10	9	∞	0	1	1·11	0·9
0·8	10	8	∞	0	2	2·5	1·6
0·7	10	7	∞	0	3	4·28	2·1
0·6	10	6	∞	0	4	6·67	2·4
0·5	10	5	∞	0	5	10	2·5
0·4	10	4	∞	0	6	15	2·4
0·3	10	3	∞	0	7	23·3	2·1
0·2	10	2	∞	0	8	40	1·6
0·1	10	1	∞	0	9	90	0·9
1	9	9	90	0·9	0	0	0
1	8	8	40	1·6	0	0	0
1	7	7	23·3	2·1	0	0	0
1	6	6	15	2·4	0	0	0
1	5	5	10	2·5	0	0	0
1	4	4	6·67	2·4	0	0	0
1	3	3	4·28	2·1	0	0	0
1	2	2	2·5	0·9	0	0	0
1	1	1	1·11	0·9	0	0	0
1	0	0	0	0	0	0	0
0·3	6	3	∞	0	3	10	0·9
0·6	3	3	10	0·9	0	0	0

the previous calculations. In the third part of the table two typical conditions are given. If the drop across R_1 alone is not sufficient then R_3 comes into operation, whereas if the drop across R_1 alone is greater than required R_2 comes into operation.

It will be seen that, when the dissipation in R_2 is large, that in R_3 is small, and vice versa. Thus when these resistors are replaced by transistors it is possible to mount them on the same heat sink.

Two possible arrangements of transistors using this principle are given in Fig. 6.31. Consider circuit (*a*) with a control signal such that TR_2 is fully conducting. The voltage V_B of the battery B is made of such a value that, under these conditions, TR_1 is fully conducting; i.e. V_B is equal to the drop across TR_2 (when bottomed) plus the base–emitter voltage of TR_1 (say 2 V total). Hence R_1 is short-circuited by TR_1 and the drop in TR_2 is small. The total regulating unit voltage is therefore small. As the control signal is reduced, i.e. the base current of TR_2 is reduced, the voltage between collector and emitter of TR_2 rises. However, any slight rise of voltage is fed to TR_1 in such a direction as to reduce the base–emitter voltage of TR_1, so increasing the voltage across it. Hence, as the

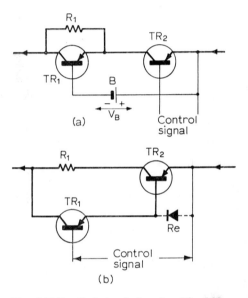

Fig. 6.31 Practical circuits based on Fig. 6.30

control signal is reduced, the voltage across TR_1 rises and less current flows in it and more current flows in R_1. This action continues until TR_1 is cut off and all the current flows in R_1. Thus, over this range of control voltage, the effective resistance of TR_1 is changed from almost zero to infinity. Power is therefore shared between the parallel elements R_1 and TR_1 in the manner already explained. The voltage across TR_2 will be small during the whole of this time, since the maximum change of voltage can only equal the normal base–emitter drop of TR_1. If the control signal is reduced further then the voltage across TR_2 rises (so maintaining TR_1

cut off) and effectively R_1 and TR_2 are in series. The power is now shared between R_1 and TR_2 in the way already explained. The battery is normally replaced by a Zener diode.

The action of the circuit shown in Fig. 6.31 (*b*) is similar. If TR_1 is made heavily conducting then TR_2 must also be heavily conducting, as the emitter current of TR_1 is the base current of TR_2 (neglecting the effect of the rectifier Re). As the control signal is reduced the voltage across TR_1 rises, less current flows through it and more flows through R_1. Thus effectively R_1 and TR_1 are in parallel and share the power between them. As the control signal is reduced a point is reached where the emitter current of TR_1 is not large enough to maintain TR_2 fully conducting, but at this point the current in TR_1 will be small compared with that in R_1. As the control signal is reduced further the voltage across TR_2 rises and effectively TR_2 and R_1 are in series and sharing the power. The rectifier Re is added to bypass part of the emitter current of TR_1 so that an excessive base current does not flow in TR_2. It has been shown by McPherson (Ref. 11) that this is a special case of the more general arrangement of a number of transistors operating in sequence in this way, all the circuits having series resistors of different values.

The advantages of using these circuits are that the transistors and heat sinks can be smaller for a given regulating unit power. Also, since most of the power is dissipated in resistors, the circuit will probably be more reliable than if all the power were dissipated in transistors.

EFFECT OF VARIABLE OUTPUT VOLTAGE ON TRANSISTOR DISSIPATION

In the last section the dissipation of the series-transistor regulating unit was considered when the output voltage was fixed. In this case the input voltage is designed to be such that under the worst operating conditions there is sufficient voltage across the series transistor for satisfactory operation but no more than necessary. For example, in a 50 V 1 A supply the voltage drop across the series transistor (on full load) may be 5 V, in which case the power dissipated in the transistor is 5 W, or 10 per cent of the maximum output power. If the output voltage is to be variable from 0 to 50 V and the same rectifier voltage is used, then under the condition of zero output voltage at full current, the drop in the series transistor is 55 V and the dissipation 55 W, or 110 per cent of the maximum stabilizer output power. This arrangement is possible with small power supplies, but with larger ones the dissipation in the series transistor becomes excessive.

One common method is to use a tapped transformer to feed the rectifier. The output voltage is varied in steps by a switched potential divider across the output (which feeds the measuring unit), and this is ganged with a switch selecting appropriate voltages from the transformer. A fine voltage adjustment is also used so that the output voltage may be varied over the range between each step. In this way the dissipation of the series transistor is considerably reduced. For the 50 V 1 A supply the arrangement might be as in Table 6.5.

TABLE 6.5

Range	Rectified voltage (full load)	Voltage across transistor	Maximum transistor dissipation
V	V	V	W
0–10	15	5–15	15
10–20	25	5–15	15
20–30	35	5–15	15
30–40	45	5–15	15
40–50	55	5–15	15

This results in a considerable reduction in power dissipation but has the disadvantage that the output has to be varied in steps rather than continuously.

Another method is to use a variable-ratio transformer such as a Variac to feed the rectifier transformer, and to gang this with the variable potential divider across the output. Variable-ratio transformers are expensive, and this idea does not appear to be used to any extent.

In both of the above methods the voltage across the series transistor is more than necessary for most of the time. In the case of the tapped transformer a compromise has to be reached between a large number of transformer taps and large transistor dissipation. In both methods the voltage across the transistor will vary with variation of supply voltage, and no correction can be made for this.

PRE-REGULATORS

A better arrangement is to use a pre-regulator, the principle of which is shown in Fig. 6.32. At (*a*) is shown the use of a variable-ratio transformer before the rectifier transformer. The variable-ratio transformer is controlled by the voltage drop across the series transistor TR_1. Thus, if the voltage across the series transistor rises above a predetermined value, the

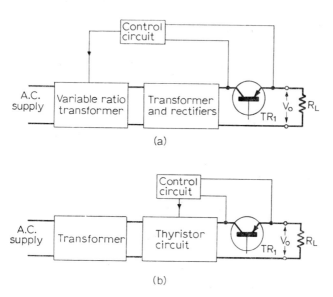

FIG. 6.32 Use of pre-regulator

(*a*) With variable-ratio transformer   (*b*) With thyristor circuit

control circuit operates so that the output voltage of the rectifiers is decreased, so as to decrease the voltage across the transistor. If the voltage across the transistor drops below some lower predetermined value, the control operates the variable-ratio transformer to increase the rectifier voltage and so raise the voltage across the transistor. One may consider that the transistor and normal stabilizer circuit take care of small rapid variations of voltage, and that the variable-ratio transformer takes care of larger voltage variations which normally take place relatively slowly. Using this principle, very large stabilized power-supply units can be manufactured, and there are commercial stabilizers using this principle

95

having an output of 500 kW with currents up to 2 000 A. These use a large number of transistors in parallel, the transistors being water cooled. A Brentford variable-ratio transformer is used to feed the rectifier transformer.

An alternative arrangement is shown in Fig. 6.32 (*b*). The variable input voltage to the stabilizer is obtained either by using silicon controlled rectifiers, or *thyristors*, in place of normal rectifiers or after the rectifiers. Again the voltage across the series transistor is used to control the "firing" of the thyristors so that an approximately constant voltage is maintained across the transistor. The thyristor pre-regulator will be more rapid acting than the variable-ratio transformer but not as rapid as the series transistor. Therefore the series transistor takes care of small rapid variations of voltage and the thyristor takes care of slower and larger ones.

When a pre-regulator is used the output voltage is varied by means of the normal potential divider associated with the measuring unit, and the rectified voltage will change so that the voltage across the series transistor remains approximately constant. Hence the output voltage can now be varied continuously over the full range rather than in steps, as previously, using a tapped transformer. The use of a pre-regulator has the advantage that the stabilized power supply can be resistance programmed (see later in chapter for more details), and this is not possible if a tapped transformer is used. There are also advantages under conditions of overload and short-circuit which are considered later. The performance of the stabilizer is also improved by the use of a pre-regulator. This is because, for variations of mains voltage or load, the pre-regulator tends to maintain a constant input voltage to the main stabilizer, and hence it has only to cope with small variations of rectified voltage.

OVERLOAD AND SHORT-CIRCUIT PROTECTION

A transistor connected in series with the load (as is normal) is very vulnerable to damage by overload or short-circuit of the output terminals. Damage may be caused for three reasons:

(*a*) Excessive voltage between collector and emitter
(*b*) Excessive collector current
(*c*) Excessive dissipation

(*a*) If the output terminals are short-circuited then the full rectified voltage is applied across the transistor. The rectifier voltage under this condition will be less than normal owing to the increased current. If the transistor has been chosen to withstand only the normal difference between input and output voltage, it will be damaged owing to excess voltage. Damage due to this cause can be avoided by the use of a transistor with a collector–emitter voltage rating in excess of the rectified voltage. This, of course, increases the cost, and in any case the transistor may be damaged owing to excessive dissipation (see (*c*) below).

(*b*) Taking an excessive current from the supply may cause damage by exceeding the current rating of the transistor. Short-circuit of the output terminals is the extreme case. The short-circuit current will be determined by the internal resistance of the rectifier circuit.

(*c*) Under moderate overload conditions the dissipation may be greater or less than normal, as explained earlier, depending on the regulation of the rectifier circuit. However, under short-circuit conditions, the dissipation will be large as the full output of the rectifier circuit is being fed into the transistor. Exactly what this dissipation will be depends on the circuit. The effect of the voltage stabilizer circuit is to tend to maintain a constant output voltage, but at some value of output current this action must fail and the voltage must drop eventually to zero on short-circuit. The maximum current that can flow is the short-circuit current of the rectifier, but in general it will be rather less than this. However, since the current will be greater than full load and the voltage across the transistor will be greater than normal, the dissipation will be excessive. In some circuits, e.g. the simple emitter follower, the current is limited because, once the base current exceeds the current in the resistor feeding the Zener diode, the latter effectively becomes open-circuited and the output voltage drops rapidly. The current may be limited in this way, but of course this results in the voltage across the transistor rising. Thus exactly what happens on overload or short-circuit depends on the circuit values, but the transistor is likely to be damaged owing to either excessive voltage or dissipation.

In valve stabilizers, protection is usually possible by the use of a fuse in the rectifier output, since a valve will normally withstand excess anode voltage and excess dissipation for the short time required to blow the fuse. However, a transistor is damaged almost instantly by excess voltage, and owing to its low heat mass, very rapidly by excess dissipation. In general, the transistor cannot be protected by a fuse as it will be damaged before the fuse clears the circuit. A high-speed relay may be used in a similar way (or by the voltage across the transistor, this being excessive on overload), but again it is doubtful whether the relay could operate quickly enough. The relay must be of a type which is manually reset and must be reset *after* the cause of the overload has been removed.

Since it is essential to have some protection (unless one is prepared to replace the series transistor and possibly other transistors every time an overload takes place), some electronic device must be used. One method

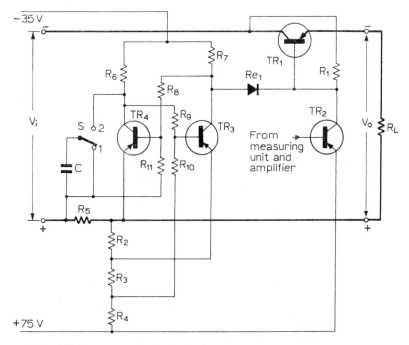

FIG. 6.33 Current-overload trip circuit

is to use an electronic trip which cuts off the series transistor until the trip is reset manually, after the cause of overload has been removed. In this case the transistor must be able to withstand the full no-load voltage of the rectifier circuit without damage, since, under short-circuit conditions, this voltage will appear across the transistor.

One type of trip circuit is shown in Fig. 6.33, where TR_1 is the series transistor controlled by transistor TR_2, fed from the measuring unit. Transistors TR_3 and TR_4 form the trip circuit, which is a bistable multivibrator circuit. Under no-load condition the base of TR_4 is connected to its emitter by R_{11} (since there will be no voltage across R_5 on no load) and is also fed with a negative voltage through R_8 from the collector of TR_3. Hence TR_4 will be conducting. The base of TR_3 is fed from a negative voltage through R_9, from the collector of TR_4, but also with a positive voltage from the potential divider R_2, R_3, R_4, through R_{10}. By suitable choice of component values the base of TR_3 is therefore positive with respect to its emitter and hence is cut off. The collector of TR_3 is therefore almost at $-35\,V$ and the rectifier Re_1 is reverse biased and non-conducting. Resistor R_5 is of low value and in series with the load, so that, as the load current increases, the voltage across R_5 increases making the base of TR_4 less negative (i.e. feeding a positive voltage through R_{11}). At a certain predetermined value of current, TR_4 becomes cut off. Its collector voltage rises, causing the base of TR_3 to go negative (through R_9) and TR_3 to become heavily conducting. Thus, the collector voltage of TR_3 drops, causing the base of TR_4 to go more positive and maintain it cut off. Since the drop across TR_3 will be small its collector will be almost at the same voltage as its emitter, i.e. that of the junction between R_2 and R_3 of the potential divider. Hence the collector changes in voltage from a negative to a positive value with respect to the positive output terminal. This causes rectifier Re_1 to conduct and change the base voltage of TR_1 to almost the same positive voltage. Since TR_1 is connected as an emitter follower the emitter and output voltage fall to zero and TR_1 is cut off. The full $35\,V$ (plus the voltage across R_2 less the drop in TR_3 and Re_1) will now be present between collector and base of TR_1, and this transistor must have a rating such that it will withstand this voltage.

To reset the device (after removing the cause of overload), switch S is moved momentarily to position 2. This connects capacitor C_2 between the collector of TR_4 and the positive input terminal and causes a momentary drop in voltage across TR_4. This causes TR_3 to cut off (since the base goes positive), and by the normal multivibrator action, causes TR_4 to become fully conducting, and hence the circuit is returned to normal. Returning switch S (normally a spring-loaded push switch) to position 1 discharges C ready for the next time. The speed of operation of this circuit is relatively rapid, say 1 ms, and will normally protect the transistor. If the reset button is pressed before the cause of overload has been removed, damage may be done, as the capacitor C tends to prevent the circuit operating correctly.

Trip circuits of this type tend to be a nuisance since they are operated by momentary surges and sometimes when the circuit is switched on. In these circumstances it is often not possible to switch on a device which takes a large starting current (such as a metal-filament lamp), even when the operating current is much less than normal full load. The protective mechanism is, of course, operating correctly under these conditions as the transistor would be overloaded, but as will be seen later, some type of current-limiting circuit is much more convenient. For these reasons trip circuits of this type are not commonly used in modern power supplies.

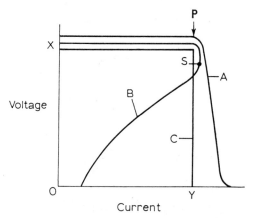

FIG. 6.34 Characteristics of overload protection circuits

Current-limiting circuits may have one of three basic characteristics as shown in Fig. 6.34. In type A the voltage remains constant until the current reaches a predetermined value indicated by P. When the current exceeds this value the voltage drops rapidly, reaching zero with a short-circuit. Under short-circuit conditions the current is rather greater than that at P, but from P to short-circuit the current is approximately constant.

In type B the voltage is again constant up to point P, but if a current greater than this is drawn from the stabilizer, the voltage drops rapidly but the current also decreases so that the characteristic is re-entrant. Under short-circuit conditions the current is much less than that at P, say 30 per cent of the value at P. This characteristic is sometimes called a "fold-back characteristic". The exact shape of curve depends on the design.

In type C the voltage remains constant up to the current indicated by P but if the load resistance is reduced further, the voltage drops and the load current remains constant. In other words, the stabilizer acts as a constant-voltage supply from X to P, but as a constant-current supply from P to Y. The change-over from constant voltage to constant current may be made very sharp, and the accuracy of maintenance of constant current may be high. This type is sometimes known as constant-voltage/ constant-current or automatic cross-over supply.

The effect on the series transistor of a short-circuit will now be considered. Assuming that there is no pre-regulator, in all cases the series transistor must withstand the full rectified voltage. The actual rectified voltage will be slightly different in the three cases, as in A it is the rectified voltage on rather more than full load (assuming for simplicity that P corresponds to full load), while in B it is the voltage at, say, 30 per cent full load, and in C the voltage on full load. With characteristic A the dissipation in the transistor is large since this is the product of the current at short-circuit multiplied by the rectified voltage at this current. Thus the transistor must be able to dissipate a power of the same order as the full-load output of the power supply. With characteristic B, the dissipation on short-circuit is less since it is now the product of the current at short-circuit (say 30 per cent full load) multiplied by the rectified voltage at this current. Depending on the particular characteristic, it may be greater than this at other parts of the characteristic; e.g. it may be greater at operating point S. The condition of maximum dissipation must therefore be determined and a transistor chosen that will dissipate this maximum figure without damage. In case C the dissipation is the full-load current multiplied by the rectified voltage at full load.

Characteristic B has the advantage that the dissipation in the device being fed from the power supply will be less than when fed from a power supply having characteristic A or C. This may be useful in experimental laboratories as the power supply tends to protect the circuit under investigation as well as itself. However, the characteristic may cause difficulties when used with devices having a large initial current. With a lamp load the power supply may not give sufficient current to heat up the filament in order that its resistance may increase and reduce the current. Thus a state of deadlock may result with little current flowing in the lamp. This is illustrated in Fig. 6.35, where a typical tungsten-filament lamp characteristic is shown. When the lamp is cold the filament takes an excessive current and the power supply is overloaded and reaches a point A, which is the intersection of the two characteristics. Although the normal operating point is C (without overload), this point will never be reached because of the intersection of the characteristics, and the operating point will remain indefinitely at A.

The point P in Fig. 6.34 corresponding to the current limit is normally variable and need not correspond to the full-load current but may be any current less than that at full load.

Characteristics A and C are similar, the difference being the order of accuracy of the constant current. The current limiting is done by using a series resistor, the voltage across it being used to feed a signal to the series transistor whenever it exceeds a predetermined value. Thus, as the current rises, the drop across the resistor increases, which tends to cut off the

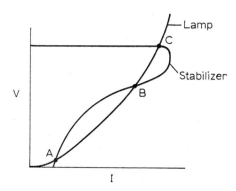

FIG. 6.35 Operation of lamp on stabilizer with overload characteristic B

series transistor and so restores the current to approximately a constant value. Essentially the circuit consists of a measuring unit across the series resistor, and hence the stabilizing circuit tends to maintain a constant voltage across the resistor. In case C the operation of the constant-current circuit is more precise.

The current-limiting circuit must be so connected that it is able to override the constant-voltage circuit. This is essential because as soon as the current limit comes into operation the voltage falls, and hence the voltage-measuring unit tends to increase the output. The principle of overriding is shown in Fig. 6.36. Below the preset current there is no output from the current-limiting circuit and hence transistor TR_3 is cut off. If the voltage tends to fall then the voltage-measuring unit causes the base of TR_2 to be less negative, so reducing the current in TR_2. As a result the drop in R_1 falls and hence the base potential of TR_1 rises and so does the output voltage. This is the action which occurs when the current is below the preset current-limiting value and the voltage is maintained constant in the normal manner. When the current tends to exceed the preset value, the base of TR_3 goes negative making TR_3 conduct, causing an increased drop in R_1 and reducing the base potential of TR_1 and also the output voltage. Thus any tendency for the current to increase causes the output voltage to decrease so as to maintain an almost constant current. When the voltage drops the voltage-measuring unit will give a large output but in such a direction as to cut off TR_2. Hence this does not interfere with the operation of the current limit. Thus the current limit operates by making TR_3 conduct, which results in TR_2 being cut off by the voltage-measuring unit. If the circuit operation had been the reverse way then, when the current limit operated so to cut off TR_3, TR_2 would conduct heavily and defeat the operation of the current limit, i.e. the current limit would not be able to override the voltage control.

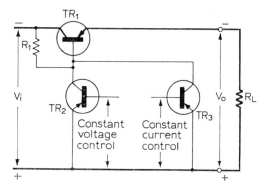

Fig. 6.36 Principle of overriding current control

The above arrangement gives characteristic A or C. When characteristic B is required a current-limiting circuit is used which at first limits the current and causes a reduction in voltage. The circuit is then arranged so that the drop in voltage causes a second circuit to reduce the voltage still further. There is positive feedback so that the voltage rapidly drops to a low value on overload.

When a pre-regulator is used the series transistor voltage is limited, provided that the pre-regulator is rapid acting as, for example, when s.c.r.s are used. With an overload the voltage across the series transistor rises and hence a signal is transmitted to the s.c.r.s to reduce the rectified voltage. On short-circuit the output voltage of the rectifiers is small and hence the dissipation of the series transistor is also small compared with the case of no pre-regulator.

OTHER PROTECTIVE FEATURES

In Fig. 6.37 is shown a basic stabilizer power supply with series transistor TR_1, fed from the two rectifiers Re_1 and Re_2. C_1 is the normal reservoir capacitor, and C_2 is a capacitor often placed across the output to reduce the output impedance at high frequencies. This may sometimes be electrolytic as shown. Under certain conditions a reverse voltage may be produced across the output terminals. One such case is shown, where two power supplies are used in series to produce a higher voltage. If power supply 2 is on and power supply 1 is off, then supply 2 is trying to force current

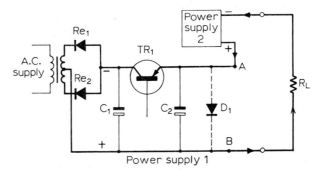

Fig. 6.37 Protection by use of diode across output terminals

through the stabilizer in the direction shown, which results in terminal A becoming positive with respect to B (i.e. the reverse polarity to normal). This results in a reverse voltage across C_2, which may damage it. Damage may also be done to TR_1 (depending on the exact circuit details and the magnitude of the voltage). To prevent this a diode D_1 may be connected across the output terminals as shown. Under normal operating conditions, i.e. A negative with respect to B, the diode is reverse biased and hence has no effect. However, if the voltage between A and B is reversed, D_1 conducts and prevents any appreciable rise in voltage across the output terminals. In the case shown the current flows in the diode and the voltage across it will be less than 1 V.

Another case where damage may be done is shown in Fig. 6.38, where two power supplies are connected in parallel in order to obtain a higher output current. Further consideration to the problem of connecting power supplies in parallel is given later. Again there are difficulties when one power supply is on and the other is off, since the two cannot be switched on and off at exactly the same instant. Suppose that power supply 2 is on and 1 is off, so that normal polarity is now applied across the output terminals. This voltage is now applied to C_1 and TR_1 in series. Since C_1 is not charged and has no voltage across it, the whole voltage is initially applied to TR_1 in the reverse direction to normal. This may damage TR_1 owing to excessive reverse base–emitter voltage. Note that no current will flow in the rectifier circuit since the rectifiers are reverse biased.

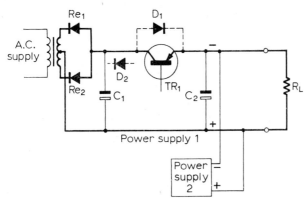

FIG. 6.38 Use of diode to protect series transistor

The risk of damage to TR_1 may be removed by connecting a diode D_1 in parallel with it, as shown. Under normal operating conditions this diode is reversed biased and has no effect. Under the conditions shown the circuit is completed through D_1, and C_1 charges rapidly to the voltage applied across the terminals. The reverse voltage across the transistor is now limited to less than 1 V. An alternative is to connect a diode, D_2, in series with TR_1. Normally this is conducting and will add a negligibly small drop in the circuit. However, under the conditions shown, it prevents a reverse current from producing an excessive reverse voltage across TR_1.

CROWBAR CIRCUIT

In some applications it is essential that the output voltage of the power supply should not rise above its normal value *under any conditions*. This is particularly important where the power supply is feeding integrated circuits. An excess voltage, even for a brief instant, may destroy hundreds of integrated circuits. Obviously the output voltage may increase owing to a fault in the stabilizer circuit, for example, because of a short-circuit of the series transistor. Even if the transistors are liberally rated there is always the possibility of this happening. Many other faults in the measuring unit and amplifier circuit could cause a voltage rise.

The stabilizer must also prevent an excess voltage due to external causes. For example, a complex piece of equipment may have voltages fed to it of different values. A short-circuit between the higher-voltage supply and the lower-voltage supply must not cause the lower-voltage supply to rise appreciably.

It is also important that the output voltage should not rise momentarily when switching off. Exactly what happens in a stabilizer circuit when switching off is not always obvious, but the voltage may rise (owing to different time-constants in the circuit), particularly on light loads. This difficulty may be overcome by using two switches, one switching off the mains and one isolating the output terminals from the stabilizer. The mains should be switched on first and switched off last. However, it is better to design the circuit to avoid this difficulty of excess voltage on switching off (and switching on), since sooner or later the switches will be operated in the incorrect order.

The circuit used to prevent rise of voltage is known as a *crowbar circuit* and is arranged to short-circuit the output terminals if the voltage rises slightly. This obviously prevents any further rise of voltage and rapidly reduces the voltage to zero. If the power supply is fitted with a current-limiting circuit, no damage is done and only the current allowed by the current-limit control flows under short-circuit conditions. The same result applies to any other high-voltage supply which may be accidentally connected across the output terminals of the lower-voltage supply. The basic crowbar circuit is given in Fig. 6.39, this being connected across the output terminals of the supply to be protected. The Zener diode D_1 is fed with a suitable current through R_3. The potential divider R_1 is set so that, under normal voltage conditions, transistor TR_1 is just non-conducting and hence TR_2 and the thyristor SCR are non-conducting. If the voltage rises the base of TR_1 goes negative with respect to the emitter, and collector current flows. This causes a drop across R_2, making TR_2 conduct, and a current limited by R_5 flows in the gate circuit of the thyristor. This causes the thyristor to conduct and short-circuit the output terminals through the limiting resistor R_4. The time of operation of this circuit is very short, usually only a few microseconds. The voltage can only be restored by switching off for a brief period so that the thyristor again becomes non-conducting. The cause of operation should, of course, be determined before switching on again.

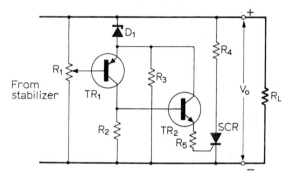

Fig. 6.39 Crowbar over-voltage protection circuit

In some special power supplies, undervoltage and undercurrent (with a normally fixed load) protection or alarm may be required.

REMOTE ERROR SENSING

A stabilized power supply gives a constant voltage at its output terminals, but if the load that it supplies is some distance away, there will be some drop in the leads and the voltage at the load will not be constant. It is not always appreciated how important this drop may be. Suppose that the equipment is situated so that the leads between the power supply and load are each 1 metre long and are of 16 s.w.g. The resistance of the two leads will be about 15 mΩ. A 2 A power supply may have an effective output resistance of only 10–20 mΩ, and hence the leads result in a drop comparable to that of the power supply. To overcome this difficulty remote sensing terminals are often fitted.

The principle is shown in Fig. 6.40. The supply is fed to the load through the main leads shown, and there will be some drop in these leads owing to their resistance. However, the measuring unit is fed through the sensing leads connected directly to the load, R_L. Since the current in these leads is small there is no appreciable drop in them, and the measuring unit is therefore fed with the voltage actually present across the load. In this way the voltage across the load is maintained constant with the same

107

accuracy as if the load were directly connected across the terminals of the power supply. Obviously there is a limit to the allowable drop in the main leads, as any such drop subtracts from the available voltage of the power supply. It is important that no voltage should be induced in the sensing leads as this would upset the accuracy, and hence they should be twisted together, or better still, screened.

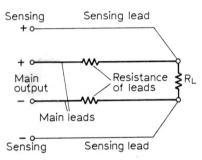

FIG. 6.40 Use of sensing leads

Normally the sensing terminals and the main terminals are joined together through a $100\,\Omega$ resistor, so that if the sensing leads become open-circuited no damage is done. If the resistors were not used then an open-circuit of the sensing leads would cause the power supply to feed the maximum available voltage to the load. When the sensing leads are not used, the measuring unit is fed through the $100\,\Omega$ resistors, but as the current is small they have a negligible effect on the output. Hence, it is normally not necessary to join the sensing and main terminals together when sensing leads are not being used. To reduce the impedance at high frequencies it may be necessary to connect a suitable capacitor across the load; otherwise the impedance of the main leads may be appreciable.

POWER SUPPLIES IN SERIES

In general, power supplies may be operated in series provided that the maximum allowable voltage to earth is not exceeded. The maximum current is, of course, that of the lowest-current supply if they are not equal. As mentioned earlier, if one power supply is switched on before the other (in practice they cannot be switched on at exactly the same instant), reverse voltage is applied to the stabilizer which is off. Thus diodes should be fitted across the output terminals to prevent damage.

POWER SUPPLIES IN PARALLEL

The operation of power supplies in parallel is more complex than their operation in series. If two constant-voltage sources are connected in parallel then one source will supply all the current and may feed current into the other source (if reversible, such as a d.c. generator). This is due to the fact that the voltages cannot be adjusted to be exactly equal and the higher-voltage source will supply all the power. The more stable the output voltages the more this action takes place. Hence, if two stabilized power supplies fitted with overload trips are connected in parallel, one power supply will generally trip out on overload (assuming the load is greater than can be supplied by one power supply).

However, with power supplies fitted with current-limiting control circuits, operation in parallel is quite satisfactory. The supplies should be adjusted until their voltages are approximately equal. The power supply with the higher voltage setting will tend to supply all the current, but when the current has risen to that settled by the current limit, the voltage will drop until it equals that of the other power supply, which then provides the additional current. The output voltage will then be that of the lower-voltage power supply.

If a constant voltage is required for a variable load (down to less than the current limit) then the voltage settings of the two power supplies should be as nearly equal as possible; otherwise there will be rise of voltage when all the current transfers to the higher-voltage supply. In general this method of operation is satisfactory, but of course the load is not shared equally by the power supplies. This is not generally important, but they can be made to share a given load equally by adjustment of the current-limit setting of the higher-voltage supply.

It was shown earlier that the application of forward voltage to a power supply not switched on may cause damage unless a diode is connected across or in series with the series transistor. It is therefore important to check this before connecting the supplies in parallel.

AUTO-TRACKING OR SLAVE OPERATION

It is sometimes desirable to have two (or more) power supplies so connected that, if the voltage of one is changed, the voltage of the other changes by the same percentage. A method of doing this is shown in Fig. 6.41. The master supply can be of any type (or any source of voltage) and does not require any modification. It is necessary, however, to bring out a special connection from the slave supply. The circuit shown is like that of Fig. 6.20 and described earlier. Normally the upper end of R_1 would be fed from the reference voltage, but it is now fed from the master supply. Since the

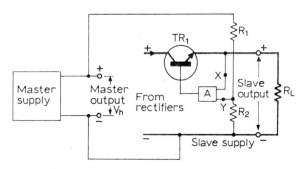

FIG. 6.41 Master and slave supply

voltage between X and Y of the amplifier A must be zero (or almost so), the output of the slave supply will be

$$V_h \frac{R_2}{R_1 + R_2}$$

where V_h is the voltage output of the master supply. Thus, as V_h is varied, the output voltage of the slave supply will always be the same fraction of it. The fraction can, of course, be changed by varying the ratio of R_1 to R_2.

RESISTANCE PROGRAMMING

It is often convenient to be able to vary the output voltage of a power supply by varying the value of an external resistor. The output voltage is made proportional to the resistance and the power supply may have a programming coefficient of say $200\,\Omega/V$. This means that if a $200\,\Omega$ external resistor is used the output voltage will be $1\,V$; if a $2\,000\,\Omega$ resistor is used the output voltage will be $10\,V$.

A stabilizer circuit which can be used in this way is shown in Fig. 6.42. The voltage reference is V_R, shown as due to a battery for convenience. The input to the amplifier A, between terminals X and Y, must be zero (or almost zero), and hence the voltage across R_1 must be equal to V_R. The current in R_1 is V_R/R_1. Assuming no current to the amplifier, the current in R_2 must be the same as that in R_1, as given above. Hence the voltage across R_2 is $(V_R/R_1)R_2$. This is the output voltage, V_o, which is evidently proportional to R_2. By suitable choice of V_R and R_1 the relationship between V_o and R_2 can be made a convenient value. The accuracy of the output voltage will depend on the accuracy and stability of R_2 and hence this must be chosen carefully.

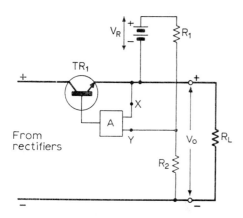

Fig. 6.42 Circuit used when resistance programming is required

Stabilized power supplies having this feature may be switched to a number of preset voltages by the use of a switch and a number of resistors. Two arrangements are shown in Fig. 6.43. The circuit at (*a*) should not be used. If the switch breaks between contacts, then infinite resistance appears in the circuit and maximum voltage is produced across the output terminals of the power supply each time the switch is operated. If the switch makes before breaking, then R_1 and R_2 are in parallel and a momentary fall in voltage results each time the switch is operated.

The correct arrangement is shown at (*b*) using a switch which makes before breaking. Thus in position 1 resistor R_1 is in circuit. When the switch is moved it will first make contact 2, but this makes no difference to the resistance in circuit. On breaking from contact 1 the new value of resistance, $R_1 + R_2$, is in circuit. The same action occurs when going from contact 2 to contact 3. Thus no transient voltages occur as with the arrangement at (*a*).

Some modifications to the power supply may be necessary if it is to be programmed rapidly. Normally, a capacitor is connected across the output terminals to reduce the output impedance at high frequencies. The rate at which the output voltage can change is limited by this capacitor. The rate of rise is limited by the charging current. The rate at which the voltage can fall is determined by the rate at which the capacitor can be discharged by the load. If the load resistance is high the rate of decrease may be quite low. Thus this capacitor may have to be removed.

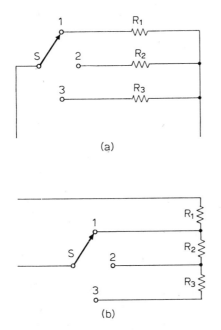

(a)

(b)

Fig. 6.43 Methods of switching resistors in resistance-programmed supply
(*a*) Incorrect   (*b*) Correct

A capacitor is sometimes connected across the upper end of the potential divider feeding the measuring unit (to increase the loop gain on a.c. and reduce the ripple). This will also tend to reduce the rate of change and may have to be removed. If a very-high-speed change is specified the stabilizer may have to be designed specially with this requirement in mind.

This resistance programming cannot be used with a power supply which requires a tapped transformer to feed the rectifiers; it can be used only where the rectifier voltage is fixed or where a pre-regulator (high speed) is used.

PIGGY BACK SUPPLY

For voltages higher than about 50 V a transistor stabilizer becomes difficult to design, and the series transistor is expensive because its voltage rating must be high. Also there is a large amount of energy stored in the reservoir capacitor, and this may damage the series transistor if a short-circuit is applied to the output terminals. These difficulties can be overcome by the use of *Piggy back* supply. The principle is shown in Fig. 6.44. The

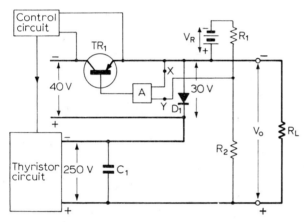

Fig. 6.44 Piggy back supply

upper portion of the circuit is a normal, say 30 V, stabilized supply, while the lower portion is, say, a 250 V supply using thyristors as rectifiers so that its output can be varied. The total output voltage is used to feed the measuring unit by connecting the potential divider R_1, R_2 across the reference voltage V_R and the total output voltage V_o. Since there must be a negligible voltage between terminals X and Y of the amplifier A, the voltage across R_1 must equal V_R, and that across R_2 must equal V_o. The total voltage is the sum of both supplies.

If the output voltage varies from its correct value a signal will be fed to TR_1 from the amplifier to correct it. However, the possible voltage variation across TR_1 is limited, and hence the voltage across TR_1 is fed to a control circuit to vary the voltage from the thyristors. Thus, if the voltage across TR_1 becomes excessive (indicating that the total input voltage is too high), the control circuit operates so as to reduce the voltage of the 250 V supply. Normally a current-limiting circuit (not shown) would be used.

113

This would tend to turn off TR_1, thus increasing the voltage across it and causing the control circuit to reduce the voltage of the 250 V supply. The diode D_1 is added so that, on short-circuit, the current of the reservoir capacitor C_1 does not flow through TR_1 and damage it. It also prevents reversal of voltage across the output terminals of the lower-voltage supply which might cause damage.

If the variations of input voltage are small, it might not be necessary to vary the voltage of the higher-voltage supply, but some method of protection would be necessary to prevent that supply being damaged by short-circuit.

OUTPUT IMPEDENCE, RESPONSE TIME, RECOVERY TIME AND TRANSIENT RESPONSE

There is considerable confusion over these terms and they are used differently by different people. In some cases the output impedance is quoted but this will vary with frequency. At low frequencies the output impedance is low owing to the action of the stabilizer, which maintains a constant voltage for a varying current. At a high frequency the stabilizer will fail to operate (owing to the limited frequency response of the amplifier), and in order to keep the output impedance low, an electrolytic capacitor is commonly connected across the output terminals. With increasing frequency the reactance of the capacitor decreases at first, but above some frequency level it effectively increases, owing to the inductance of the capacitor.

Thus the impedance, even with an electrolytic capacitor connected across the output terminals, increases at high frequencies. The impedance may be measured by superimposing an alternating voltage between the output terminals and the load, and noting the corresponding alternating current. The figures obtained may depend on the value of the load, the voltage setting and the value of alternating voltage used. The use of a sinusoidal waveform may be misleading, since load changes tend to take place in steps and not sinusoidally. Hence tests using a step change of load may be more valuable.

For simplicity it will be assumed that the load change is from full load to no load, and a typical result is shown in Fig. 6.45. When full load is removed at instant A the voltage will rise rapidly to point B and then the stabilizer will come into action to correct the output voltage, which will eventually settle down at a slightly higher value corresponding to no load,

114

as shown. The problem is to define the *recovery time*. It is roughly the time for the voltage to reach the final value it would have after making the load change. If the transient is exponential then mathematically the voltage only reaches the final value in infinite time, but one can use the idea of time-constant, i.e. the time for 63·3 per cent of the change to take place.

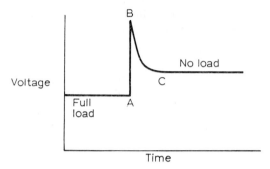

FIG. 6.45 Transient produced by switching off load

This is indicated in Fig. 6.46, where T is the recovery time, or response time. An alternative is to quote the time for the voltage to recover to within say x millivolts of its final value. Another alternative is to quote the time for the voltage to recover within x millivolts of the nominal output voltage (i.e. the voltage midway between the no-load and full-load values). A similar action will, of course, occur when the change is from no load to full load, but the transient will be in the opposite direction.

A change from full load to no load (or vice versa) has been used, but in some cases a smaller change is taken, say 10–90 per cent full load. The

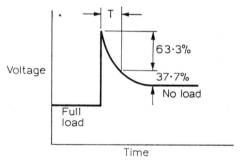

FIG. 6.46 Response time of stabilizer

115

recovery time is even more difficult to define if the transient is in the form of damped oscillation. Obviously, with all the above methods of specifying the recovery time and when different methods are used by different manufacturers, it becomes difficult to compare one power supply with another of different manufacture. If the load changes are made very rapidly then the inductance of the power supply may cause very sharp transient spikes which may be of importance, particularly in digital work. A high-speed oscillograph is necessary in order to detect these short-duration spikes.

There will also be a recovery time for sudden changes of input voltage, but this is not normally quoted. This is more complicated since it depends at which instant of the cycle of the supply the change is made. Some smoothing out of these transients is effected by the reservoir capacitor.

VOLTAGE STABILIZER MODULES

So far it has been assumed that the power supply is fed from a.c. mains and the rectifier circuit and stabilizer circuit are all part of one unit. It is sometimes convenient to separate the rectifier circuit from the stabilizer circuit, and one rectifier circuit may feed a number of stabilizer circuits. In this case the stabilizer sections are often called *modules*. They are supplied with an unstabilized direct voltage but produce a stabilized direct voltage output. The advantage of separation is that the drop in the leads can be reduced. If the stabilizer is feeding one load at a fixed point then correction for lead drop can be made by the use of sensing leads, as explained earlier. However, if the stabilizer is required to feed a number of loads through different leads, this method cannot be used.

Voltage drop in the leads can, however, be overcome by the use of voltage stabilizer modules as shown in Fig. 6.47. Provided that the module is placed near to the load, the voltage supplied to the load will be correctly stabilized. The drop in the leads to the module will have no effect, provided that it is not so large that insufficient voltage is fed to the module. The arrangement also has the advantage of isolating the loads and preventing the drop in a common lead causing feedback or interference between the various loads. The arrangement is simpler than using completely separate power supply and also prevents possible interference from the mains supply, which might occur if transformer and mains leads were placed near the loads.

The design of these modules is basically no different from that of normal stabilizer circuits. However, modules are available commercially which are very small. They may be made using discrete components on a normal printed circuit. In this case considerable dissipation is possible in the series transistor provided that a heat sink is used. The modules may also be made on printed circuits and encapsulated. They are then small and unlikely to be damaged mechanically. The dissipation is limited by the size. Another alternative is to use a thick-film circuit where the passive elements are fused onto an alumina substrate and chip semiconductors are bonded to the substrate and suitably connected. These can be made very small (e.g. $1 \times \frac{1}{2} \times 0.17$ in), but the power dissipation is obviously limited.

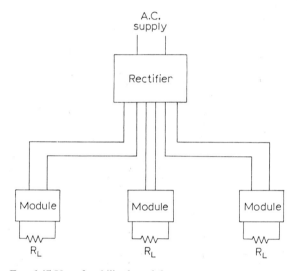

Fig. 6.47 Use of stabilized modules

In all these devices the power dissipation can be kept small by arranging that the difference between the input and output voltages is small. The latest form is the integrated circuit or monlithic voltage regulator module. In principle this is no different from the circuits already described, but because of the nature of integrated circuits, the actual circuits are different. When discrete components are used, resistors and capacitors are relatively cheap and are available in a large range of values but transistors are expensive. Hence one designs the circuit to have as few transistors as possible, and if this results in a large number of resistors this is generally satisfactory. In an integrated circuit conditions are quite different and the cost of the component tends to be directly related to the space it takes up on the chip. Thus resistors which tend to be large are expensive and only small-value capacitors are possible. Diodes and transistors are cheap since they are small. Since all the diodes and transistors are made at the same time, the number is of little importance. Thus active elements are used much more freely, and resistors, and particularly capacitors, are to be avoided.

Obviously a large number of circuit arrangements are possible; that to be described (Type L M100) is manufactured by the National Semiconductor Corporation. The basic circuit is shown in Fig. 6.48, where TR_1 is the series transistor. A fraction of the output voltage is developed across R_2 and is compared with the reference voltage V_R, so that there is a negligible voltage between the input terminals of amplifier A.

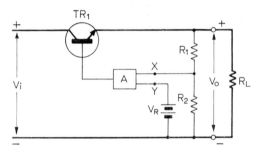

FIG. 6.48 Basic circuit of integrated-circuit voltage stabilizer

V_R is obtained from what is essentially a Zener diode. If the output voltage is to be variable, its minimum value is settled by V_R, since it cannot be less than V_R in the circuit shown in Fig. 6.48. Thus V_R should be small so that the output voltage can be varied over a considerable range. The Zener diode is formed by the emitter–base junction of a transistor using reverse-bias emitter–base breakdown. For economy all the transistors are made at the same time and therefore have similar characteristics. The same control over the characteristics cannot be obtained as when only a Zener diode is being made as a discrete component. The reverse-bias emitter–base breakdown voltage used is about 6·3 V with a temperature coefficient of $+ 2·3\,mV/°C$, and hence a method of temperature compensation is required, as shown in Fig. 6.49.

The Zener diode D_1 is fed by a constant-current source from the input to the stabilizer. The transistor TR_1 acts as an emitter follower and hence prevents loading of D_1, which operates at a very small current. In this circuit the diodes are actually transistors with collector and base joined together, i.e. using the base–emitter junction. Diodes D_2 and D_3 are used for temperature compensation. The base voltage of TR_1 increases with temperature by about $+2.3\,mV/°C$ (since D_1 has a positive temperature coefficient). The emitter voltage of TR_1 will increase more since the base–emitter drop decreases with temperature. This is increased still more by the use of D_2 (whose drop decreases with increase of temperature), so that the voltage at the lower end of D_2 has a temperature coefficient of about $+7\,mV/°C$. The voltage is now divided to produce a lower value (about $1.7\,V$) by means of R_1, R_2 and D_3. The effect of D_3 is to reduce the temperature coefficient at the tapping point almost to zero.

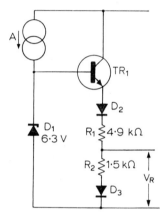

Fig. 6.49 Reference voltage supply

If one assumes the nominal base–emitter drop (and diode voltage drop) to be $0.7\,V$, the voltage at the lower end of D_2 will be $6.3 - (2 \times 0.7) = 4.9\,V$. The voltage across R_1 and R_2 is therefore this voltage less the drop across D_3, i.e. $4.9 - 0.7 = 4.2\,V$. The voltage across R_2 is then

$$\frac{R_2}{R_1 + R_2} \times 4.2 = \frac{1.5}{4.9 + 1.5} \times 4.2 = 0.99\,V$$

while that across R_1 is $4.2 - 0.99 = 3.21\,V$. Thus the voltage at the tapping point is $0.7 + 0.99 = 1.69\,V$. Suppose the temperature increases by $10°C$; then the base of TR_1 has a voltage of $6.3 + (10 \times 0.0023) = 6.323\,V$ (since D_1 has a temperature coefficient of $+2.3\,mV/°C$). The drop across the diodes is now $0.7 - (10 \times 0.003) = 0.67\,V$ (assuming a temperature coefficient of $-3\,\text{mV}/°\text{C}$). Thus the voltage across R_1 and R_2 is $6\cdot323 - (3 \times 0\cdot67) = 4\cdot313\,\text{V}$. The voltage across R_1 is $(1\cdot5/6\cdot4) \times 4\cdot313 = 1\cdot01\,\text{V}$. The voltage at the tapping point is therefore $1\cdot01 + 0\cdot67 = 1\cdot68\,\text{V}$ as compared with $1\cdot69\,\text{V}$ previously.

A simplified circuit of the stabilizer is shown in Fig. 6.50, where D_1, TR_1, D_2, D_3, R_1 and R_2 are the same components as in Fig. 6.49. Transistors TR_4 and TR_5 form a long-tailed-pair amplifier, with the base of

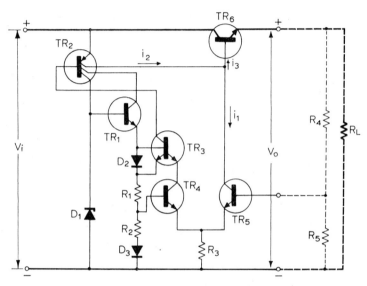

FIG. 6.50 Simplified circuit of integrated-circuit stabilizer

TR_4 fed by a constant reference voltage from across R_2 and D_3. The base of TR_5 is fed with a fraction of the output voltage V_o by the potential divider R_4, R_5, the resistors being external to the integrated circuit. The series transistor is TR_6 connected as an emitter follower. The transistor TR_2 has three collectors: one feeds the Zener diode D_1, the second feeds the emitter follower TR_1 and the third feeds transistor TR_5. The current through R_1 is divided between D_2 and one of the emitters of TR_3. By making the junction area of this emitter greater than that of D_2 (which is actually a transistor), $5/6$ of the current in R_1 flows in TR_3 and $1/6$ in D_2. The collector current of TR_3 is therefore approximately $5/6$ of the current in R_1 plus the collector current of TR_4. The collector current of TR_3 is the base current of TR_2. Since TR_3 is connected as an emitter follower (as regards TR_4) and its base is connected to a point of constant voltage (for a given temperature), TR_4 is fed with a constant collector voltage, and changes in input voltage, V_o, do not change its operating conditions.

Suppose that the output voltage rises, so causing TR_5 to take a larger current. Under normal operating conditions, a current i_3 must flow in the base of TR_6 to provide the load current, I_L. This current i_3 comes from the difference between i_2 and i_1. Thus if i_1 increases, i_3 will be reduced, which will increase the drop across TR_6 so as to restore the output voltage to its correct value. The effect of increasing the current in TR_5 is to reduce the current in TR_4 (since the current in R_3 must be approximately constant). This reduces the current in TR_3 and in the base of TR_2, so tending to reduce i_2 and increase the effective gain.

The complete circuit is shown in Fig. 6.51, where various components have been added to the circuit of Fig. 6.50. Instead of a single series transistor, a compound pair (Darlington pair) is used consisting of TR_6 and TR_7. The emitter current of TR_7 is now the base current of TR_6, and hence the change of current required in the base of TR_7, and hence in the collector of TR_5, is greatly reduced. When an external transistor, which may be necessary for larger outputs (see later), is not being used, R_6 is short-circuited by connecting terminals 3 and 2 together. A transistor TR_8 and diode D_4 (actually a transistor) are added to increase the current gain of TR_2, which, owing to the method of construction, is normally low. The current of TR_3 is now supplied partly from the base of TR_2 (through D_4) and partly from the emitter of TR_8.

In order to start the circuit it is necessary to pass a current through D_1 to bring it to its breakdown point, and this is done by the current flowing in R_9 and R_8 from the output (i.e. through the load). This current flows in the base of TR_2 (through D_4), and hence a collector current can now flow in D_1. In order to prevent variation of input voltage appearing across R_8 (and hence varying the current loading on TR_8), Zener diode D_5 is added, which maintains a constant voltage (relative to the positive line) at the junction of R_8, R_9

If current limiting is not required, R_7 is short-circuited, but of course there is then no protection of the stabilizer against overload or short-circuit. With the current limit in operation, the voltage across R_7 (plus that across R_{11}) is applied between base and emitter of TR_9. When this voltage exceeds a predetermined value (i.e. the current exceeds a certain value), TR_9 becomes conducting and tends to remove any base drive from TR_7, so tending to cut off TR_6 and reducing the output voltage and

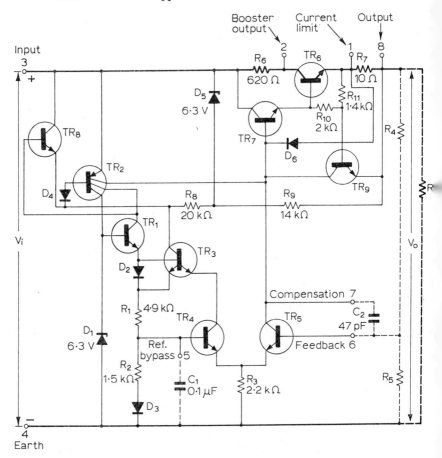

Fig. 6.51 Complete circuit of integrated-circuit stabilizer

(National Semiconductor Corporation)

current. It will be seen that TR_9 is fed, not only with the voltage across R_7, which is proportional to load current, but also with the voltage across R_{11}, which is proportional to the base–emitter drop of TR_6. This is done so that, when the dissipation is high, and the temperature of the chip is high, the value of the current limit is reduced by a factor of 2 when the temperature increases from 25°C to 150°C. This operates because the emitter current density (at the current corresponding to the current limit) is greater in TR_6 than in TR_9, and hence TR_6 has a lower negative temperature coefficient of base–emitter voltage than TR_9, Thus as the temperature rises the base–emitter drop of TR_9 decreases at a greater rate than the drop across R_{11}, and so the current limit operates at a lower current. This system will operate only if TR_6 and TR_9 are in close thermal contact and are therefore at approximately the same temperature as when on a single chip.

Diode D_6 is used only when the circuit is serving as a switching stabilizer.

An external capacitor C_1 ($0\cdot1\,\mu F$) is added to reduce the noise associated with the reference voltage applied to the base of TR_4. The external capacitor C_2 (47 pF) is added to prevent oscillation due to positive feedback at high frequencies.

The circuit will operate with an input voltage between 8·5 and 40 V and produce an output voltage between 2 and 30 V (by change of the ratio of R_4 to R_5), provided that the output/input voltage differential is between 3 and 30 V. The load regulation is 0·1 per cent and the line regulation, 0·05 %/V. The output current is limited to 12 mA, but by incorporating external transistors this may be increased to 250 mA (one transistor) or 2 A (two transistors).

The relevant portion of the circuit is shown for both cases in Fig. 6.52. At (*a*) the collector current of TR_6 is now the base current of TR_{10} (apart from the small current in R_6), and hence TR_6 controls TR_{10}, which can deal with larger powers. The value of the current-limiting resistor is reduced so that the current limit is increased appropriately. To prevent oscillation, a low-inductance (solid tantulum electrolytic) capacitor of $1\,\mu F$ must be connected across the output terminals.

At (*b*) the circuit is similar, but transistor TR_{10} is used to drive the *n-p-n* power transistor TR_{11}. Again the value of the current-limiting resistor is reduced. With this circuit it is also necessary to bypass the input terminals with a low-inductance $1\,\mu F$ capacitor, and it may be necessary to attach a ferrite bead to the emitter lead of TR_{11} to prevent oscillation. The bypass capacitor across the output is increased to $4\cdot7\,\mu F$. The performance of these larger-current circuits is similar to that of the basic circuit.

The whole integrated circuit is on a chip only 38 mil square and contained in a case of maximum diameter 0·37 in and 0·185 in high (excluding leads).

A hybrid voltage regulator is manufactured by Philco containing field-effect and bipolar transistors. The basic circuit is shown in Fig. 6.53. The load R_L is connected across points 6 and 10, and for a fixed output voltage,

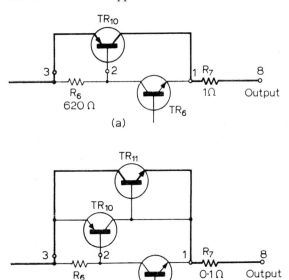

(a)

(b)

FIG. 6.52 Methods of increasing current output of circuit of Fig. 6.51

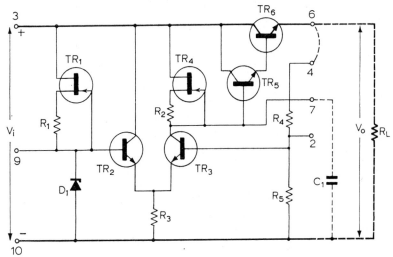

FIG. 6.53 Hybrid voltage regulator circuit
(*Philco*)

points 6 and 4 are joined together, R_4 and R_5 forming the potential divider feeding the differential amplifier (or comparison amplifier) TR_2 and TR_3. If a variable output voltage is required, the link between terminals 4 and 6 is removed and a suitable resistor connected between terminals 6 and 2. The Zener diode D_1 is fed through the field-effect transistor TR_1 with a resistor R_1 in series with the source-lead. This acts as a constant-current device so that the Zener diode current does not vary with change of supply voltage. Transistors TR_2 and TR_3 form the amplifier which compares the voltage across D_1 with a fraction of the output voltage across R_5. The field-effect transistor TR_4, with its source resistor R_2, forms the load on TR_3. Since this acts as a constant-current device the effective load on TR_3 is high. TR_3 feeds the base of TR_5, which in turn feeds the base of TR_6, the series transistor. Thus a rise in output voltage causes TR_3 to conduct more and produce a greater drop across TR_4. The base voltage of TR_5 is therefore reduced, and since TR_5 and TR_6 are connected as emitter followers, the output voltage drops to restore equilibrium. A capacitor C_1 is added externally to prevent instability.

The normal output voltage is 12 V with a maximum load regulation of 0·1 per cent and maximum line regulation of 0·02%/V. The absolute maximum output current is 200 mA. A larger output current (up to 3 A or more) can be obtained by connecting an external transistor TR_7 as in Fig. 6.54. C_1 is now increased to 5 000 pF.

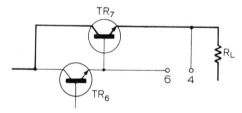

Fig. 6.54 Method of increasing output current of circuit of Fig. 6.53

Current limiting can be included with an external circuit, and a fold-back current-limiting circuit is shown in Fig. 6.55. The base of the current-limiting transistor TR_8 is now held at about + 11 V (assuming a 12 V output). On no load the emitter of TR_8 is at + 12 V, and hence TR_8 is cut off. As the current is increased the drop across the 20 Ω current-limiting resistor increases and eventually TR_8 becomes conducting. (The emitter remains at 12 V, since this is the stabilized output, and the voltage on the emitter of TR_6 rises to allow for the drop in R_8.) When TR_8 conducts it robs current from the base of TR_5 and causes the output voltage to fall. As the value of the load resistor decreases the voltage continues to fall, together with the current, and a fold-back characteristic is obtained.

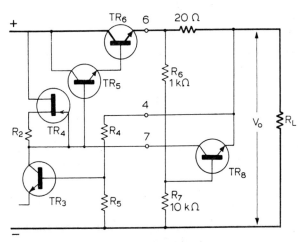

FIG. 6.55 Fold-back current-limiting circuit

Integrated circuits may also be used in stabilizer circuits which mainly use discrete components. For example, the comparison amplifier, or differential amplifier, may be an integrated circuit.

TYPICAL FIGURES

Supply	Fractional stabilization ratio, S'	Internal resistance	Ripple
			mV (p-p)
15 V 1 A: simple circuit	100	$0 \cdot 025 \, \Omega$	5
30 V 1 A: high-precision circuit			
Constant-voltage operation*	5 000–10 000	$0 \cdot 001 \, \Omega$	0·5
Constant-current operation	5 000–10 000	$0 \cdot 5$–$2 \, M\Omega$	0·5

* Temperature coefficient, 0·01 %/°C
Response time, 2–20μs (depending on how specified)

Supply	Fractional stabilization ratio, S'	Internal resistance
6 V 50 mA: simple circuit with regulating unit in parallel with load		Ω
Circuit of Fig. 6.3	20	7
Circuit of Fig. 6.6	140	6
25 V 1 A: emitter follower		
Simple circuit of Fig. 6.8	7	1·1
Constant-current circuit to feed Zener diode, as Fig. 6.10	33	0·7
Compound emitter follower with constant-current circuit to feed Zener diode, as Fig. 6.11	40	0·4
Compound emitter follower using complementary transistors and constant-current circuit to feed Zener diode, Fig. 6.14	100	0·1

7

Switching-mode Voltage Stabilizers

The stabilizers so far considered have consisted essentially of a series element, either a valve or transistor (or resistor), across which the difference between the input and output voltages is developed, and whose effective resistance is varied in order to maintain a constant output voltage. Since the input and output currents are almost the same, the series element must dissipate a power equal to the product of this current and the difference between the input and output voltages. For this reason voltage stabilizers of this type are sometimes called *dissipative stabilizers*. They have the following disadvantages:

(*a*) The efficiency is low, since the energy dissipated in the series element is lost. When the power supply is fed from the a.c. mains, the rectified voltage can be made any desired value (by the use of a transformer of suitable ratio), and hence the difference between the input and output voltages can be kept small, so that the efficiency is reasonably high. However, if the stabilizer is fed from a d.c. source of considerably higher voltage than the output, the efficiency is low. This occurs, particularly in earth satellites, where a number of stabilized voltages are required, all being obtained from a common supply. Since the power available in a satellite is very limited, the low efficiency of dissipative power supplies cannot be tolerated, particularly if the stabilized output voltage is much less than that of the d.c. supply available.

(*b*) There are difficulties in dissipating the power in the series element, particularly in satellites, when large powers are concerned. Thus large heat sinks have to be used and the stabilizer becomes large and heavy.

Ideally, then, some series element is required which will not have to dissipate appreciable power, and this can be achieved by using a series element which is alternatively fully on and completely off. When it is fully on there is no power dissipated because, although it is passing current there is no voltage drop across it (in practice there will be a small drop and small dissipation). When the device is off there is no current and hence no dissipation. In other words, the series element is basically a switch which is closed and opened rapidly. The mean current and power fed through the series element can be varied by varying the time the switch is closed relative to the time that it is open. In fact the device is being *pulse-width modulated*.

A valve is not of much use for the series element because, even when fully on, there is a large voltage across it. A transistor, on the other hand, has only a small voltage drop when fully conducting (bottomed) and hence is ideally suited for this application. A thyristor is also suitable since again its voltage drop, when conducting , is low, but a more elaborate circuit is required to switch it off.

When the device is fully conducting, energy is fed from input to output, and when it is non-conducting there is no energy transfer. The mean power fed through the device must equal the power output of the stabilizer. Since the series element operates in bursts and the energy output to the load must be continuous, some energy storage device must be used, and there are two possible choices, the capacitor and the inductor. A capacitor cannot be used by itself, since every time a capacitor is charged there is a loss in the circuit equal to the energy stored. For example, suppose that a capacitor is charged through a resistor there must always be some resistance in the circuit and hence this always applies (unless an inductor is used), then there will be loss in the resistor due to the flow of charging current, and it can be shown that this loss is equal to the energy stored in the capacitor.

Thus an inductor together with a capacitor is used, the basic circuit being shown in Fig. 7.1. The series device is shown, for convenience, as a switch S_1. The inductor L_1 and capacitor C_1 form the energy-storage circuit. Suppose that the voltage across C_1 is constant and that the output voltage is less than the input voltage. When the switch is closed a current i flows in inductor L_1 feeding load resistor R_L, which under ideal conditions must equal the load current I_L. The current flowing in L_1 builds up a magnetic field and hence stores energy. When S_1 is opened the current in the inductor tries to continue flowing. In the circuit shown it can continue, and flows in the diode D_1, thus supplying the load during the time the switch is open. It is essential to include D_1 (sometimes known as a

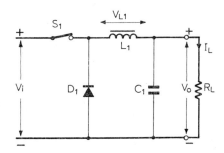

FIG. 7.1 Basic switching-mode circuit

flywheel diode), as otherwise a high voltage would be set up across the inductor, trying to force the current across the contacts of S_1. If the current i flowing in L_1 is greater than the load current, the voltage will rise as the surplus current will flow into C_1, charging it up.

In practice neither the current in the inductor nor the voltage across the capacitor is constant. When S_1 is closed the voltage across the inductor is the difference between the input and output voltages, i.e. $V_i - V_o$. If we assume a perfect inductor with no resistance then the voltage across the inductor is given by

$$V_{L1} = V_i - V_o = L_1 \frac{di}{dt} \tag{7.1}$$

Thus di/dt is determined by the value of L_1 and the voltage difference $V_i - V_o$, and during the time the switch is closed, the current will rise. If, at any instant, this current is not equal to the load current then current will flow out of C_1 to make up the difference. The relationship for the capacitor is

$$i_c = C_1 \frac{dv}{dt} \tag{7.2}$$

and hence if i_c is flowing out of the capacitor the voltage must fall at a rate determined by the magnitude of i_c and the value of C_1. If the current in the inductor exceeds the load current then the excess current will flow into the capacitor and the voltage across it will increase. As will be seen later, at the start of the period when S_1 is closed the current in L_1 is less than the load current, and at the end of the period it is greater than the load current.

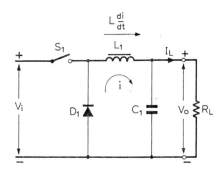

Fig. 7.2 Operation of switching-mode circuit when switch S_1 is open

If C_1 is large, so that the change of voltage across it is small, it can be assumed that $V_i - V_o$ is constant; hence, from eqn. (7.1),

$$\frac{di}{dt} = \frac{1}{L_1}(V_i - V_o) \tag{7.3}$$

or considering a change of current δ_i in the time δt that the switch is closed,

$$\delta i = \frac{\delta t}{L_i}(V_i - V_o) \tag{7.4}$$

The change of current is made small during this time δt by making L_1 large.

When the switch is opened the current in L_1 falls and a voltage is induced in it equal to $L_1 \, di/dt$, this being in such a direction as to tend to maintain the current, as shown in Fig. 7.2. Neglecting the drop in the diode D_1, the voltage must equal the output voltage V_o, i.e.

$$L_1 \frac{di}{dt} = V_o \tag{7.5}$$

131

Hence the current will fall at such a rate that the above equation is satisfied. If the time during which the switch is open is δt then the change of current δi is given by

$$\delta i = \frac{\delta t}{L_1} V_o \qquad (7.6)$$

Again the change of current δi can be made small, over this interval, by making L_1 large.

The operation is shown in more detail in Fig. 7.3. From A to B, and

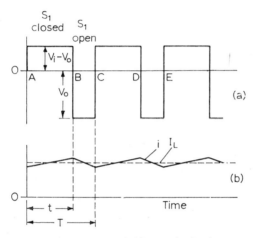

FIG. 7.3 Operation of switching-mode circuit
(*a*) Voltage across L_1 (*b*) Currents i in L_1, and I_L in load

C to D, the switch is closed, and from B to C, and D to E, it is open. It will be assumed that V_o is constant and is twice $V_i - V_o$. During the period AB the voltage across the inductor is $V_i - V_o$ and the current will rise at a rate determined by eqn. (7.3). During the period BC the switch is open so that the voltage across the inductor must equal V_o (neglecting the drop in the diode D_1), and hence the current falls at the rate determined by eqn. (7.5). Since V_o is twice $V_i - V_o$, the rate of fall of current during the period BC must be twice as great as the rate of rise during the period AB. Under equilibrium conditions (i.e. no mean fall or rise of the current in the inductor), the interval BC must be half of the interval AB. Since there is no source of energy in the circuit, other than the input, the mean current through the inductor must equal the load current, as shown in Fig. 7.3 (*b*). The difference between the current in the inductor and that in the load, at any instant, is the current flowing into or out of the capacitor C_1. The energy fed into C_1 must, of course, equal that coming out under equilibrium conditions.

The energy output of the circuit during the whole period T (the sum of "on" and "off" times) will be $I_L V_o T$. The energy input during the interval when S_1 is closed (i.e. AB) must be $I_L V_i t$. Since there is no other source of energy in the circuit, and neglecting any losses other than in the load,

$$I_L V_o T = I_L V_i t$$

i.e. energy output must equal energy input, whence

$$\frac{t}{T} = \frac{V_o}{V_i} \tag{7.7}$$

The fraction of the total time that the switch is closed, t/T, is known as the *duty cycle*. Thus under equilibrium conditions the ratio of output voltage to input voltage must equal the duty cycle. Put another way,

$$V_o = V_i \frac{t}{T}$$

and hence V_o can be varied, or maintained constant with varying V_i by varying the duty cycle, which corresponds to pulse-width modulation.

It will be seen that ideally the circuit is 100 per cent efficient whatever the ratio of output voltage to input voltage. In practice the efficiency is less than this but is nevertheless much higher than in the dissipative circuit. There will be some loss in the switch since, if a transistor or silicon controlled rectifier is used, even when fully conducting there will be a finite drop across it which is usually only a fraction of a volt. There will also be a finite loss in the inductor since it must have some ohmic resistance. The core loss is likely to be small in comparison. The flywheel diode D_1 also introduces loss when the current flows in it during the time when the switch is off. The duty cycle may be varied in one of two ways:

(*a*) The time T (and therefore the frequency) can be maintained constant and t can be varied.

(*b*) The "on" time t may be maintained constant and the "off" time varied. This means that the total time T and hence the frequency is varied.

Both methods of operation are used.

The simplest circuits are those using transistors, since a transistor is easily switched on and off by a suitable pulse waveform on its base. The basic principles of one arrangement are given in Fig. 7.4, where TR_1 is the

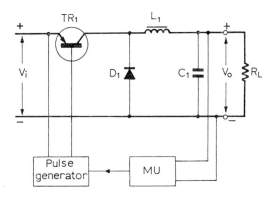

FIG. 7.4 Switching-mode stabilizer circuit

switching transistor; L_1 and C_1 form the energy storage circuit; and D_1 is the flywheel diode. The transistor is fed from the pulse generator, which is controlled by the measuring unit MU connected across the output. If the output voltage rises, then a signal is fed from the measuring unit to reduce the width of the "on" pulse from the pulse generator. In this case the frequency is maintained constant by the pulse generator and the pulses are pulse-width modulated by the measuring unit.

The frequency of the pulse generator is commonly 10–20 kHz but may be lower. The frequency has to be a compromise between a number of conflicting requirements. The higher the frequency the greater is the loss in the switching transistor TR_1. This is because every time the transistor is switched on or off there is a power loss, since the time of switching is finite. During switching a current flows through the transistor and there is also a relatively large voltage across it. Thus the greater the number of times it is switched the greater is the loss, for a given transistor. Some improvement can be obtained by increasing the speed of switching (by the design of the pulse generator) and by using a suitable transistor TR_1. The higher the frequency the smaller can be the values of L_1 and C_1 for a given ripple in the output voltage. Also, the higher the frequency the faster is the response, since correction can only be made between one pulse and the next. The pulse generator may be a self-oscillator which determines the pulse frequency, or it may operate at the supply frequency if the device is being fed off an a.c. supply. With a 50 Hz supply the frequency is often too low.

There are a number of methods of producing pulse-width modulation of the switching signal, and a simple one is shown in Fig. 7.5. The control

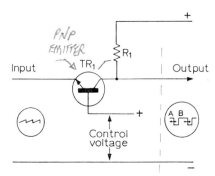

Fig. 7.5 Method of pulse-width modulation

voltage from the measuring unit drives the base of the modulating transistor TR_1. The emitter of TR_1 receives a sawtooth waveform in a positive direction. Suppose that the control voltage is 2 V on the base of TR_1. At the start of the sawtooth waveform TR_1 will be cut off, since the emitter is at zero voltage. TR_1 will switch on when the sawtooth waveform is equal to the base voltage plus the base–emitter drop, say 2·5 V.

When the transistor conducts the collector voltage will go in a negative direction and produce the edge A of the output pulse. At the end of the sawtooth waveform the transistor will cut off again and the collector voltage will rise to the supply voltage, corresponding to the other edge, B, of the output pulse. If now the control voltage on the base of TR_1 is, say, 3 V, then the sawtooth waveform will have to reach 3·5 V (assuming $V_{BE} = 0\cdot5$ V) before TR_1 becomes conducting so that the edge A is delayed and the width of the pulse (AB) is reduced. Thus, as the control voltage is varied, the edge A of the pulse moves backwards and forwards.

If a triangular waveform is used instead of a sawtooth waveform, then both sides of the pulse are moved as in Fig. 7.6. Thus, when the control voltage corresponds to V_{c1} the transistor is switched on at instant A and off at instant B. When the control voltage is V_{c2} it is switched on at A' and off at B'. Again, pulse-width modulation results.

135

A similar action takes place if a sine wave is used in place of the triangular wave, but then the pulse width is not linearly related to the control voltage. This disadvantage is not particularly important in this application, especially if a large range of pulse widths is not required. The circuit, of course, requires a suitable waveform generator to feed the modulating transistor.

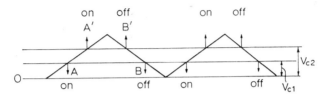

FIG. 7.6 Use of triangular wave for pulse-width modulation

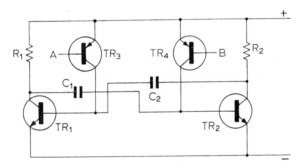

FIG. 7.7 Pulse-width modulation of multivibrator

An alternative is to modulate the pulse generator directly. One method is shown in Fig. 7.7. The transistors TR_1, TR_2 together with R_1, R_2, C_1, C_2 form a multivibrator (self-running or astable type). The normal charging resistors to the bases have been replaced by transistors TR_3 and TR_4. The effective resistances of these transistors can be varied by varying the voltages on the bases. The time of one half-cycle of the multivibrator is determined by the product of C_1 and the effective resistance of TR_4, while the time of the other half-cycle is determined by the product of C_2 and the effective resistance of TR_3. If the frequency is to be maintained constant, the time of one half-cycle must be decreased by the same amount as that of the other half-cycle is increased. This can be achieved by feeding the bases of

136

TR_3 and TR_4 with what might be termed a push-pull signal; i.e. as the base of TR_3 is made more negative, that of TR_4 must be made more positive.

These control voltages can be obtained from a long-tailed pair as in Fig. 7.8. The base of TR_6 is fed with a fixed voltage from the potential divider R_5, R_6. If the control voltage on the base of TR_5 is made more positive the collector current of TR_5 will increase, while that of TR_6 will

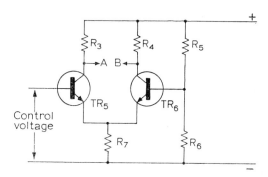

FIG. 7.8 Circuit to feed modulating transistors of Fig. 7.7

decrease by almost the same amount (since the current in R_7 is almost fixed as the voltage across it must always be approximately that across R_6). Thus point A (and hence the base of TR_3 of Fig. 7.7) will become less positive, while point B (and hence the base of TR_4) will become more positive.

If a change of frequency is not important then only one of the control transistors of Fig. 7.7 may be used. In this case the "on" time is changed while the "off" time remains constant, as shown in Fig. 7.9. Thus the "on" time AB is varied but the "off" time BC remains fixed. Obviously this results in a change in the duration of a cycle and hence in the frequency, but in some applications this may not be important.

An alternative arrangement is to obtain the switching action from the stabilizer circuit itself, and one example is given in Fig. 7.10. TR_1, D_1, L_1 and C_1 form the normal components of the switching circuit. The measuring unit consists of the Zener diode D_2 fed from resistor R_1. Suppose that TR_1 is conducting and passing a current through L_1. This will cause the voltage across C_1 and hence the voltage across R_1 to rise. At a certain predetermined value the Schmitt trigger circuit will be triggered and switch

137

off the drive to TR_1, so cutting it off. Current will continue to flow in L_1 and D_1, but the voltage across C_1, and hence across R_1, will now decrease. Eventually the voltage across R_1 will fall to such a value that the trigger circuit switches off and hence turns on TR_1 again. Thus the circuit continually switches on and off in this way.

If the load current is small then, when TR_1 is on, the rate of rise of voltage across C_1 (and hence R_1) is relatively rapid, and hence TR_1 is soon switched off. However, the rate of fall of voltage across C_1, now that TR_1 is off, will be low and hence TR_1 will remain off for a relatively long time.

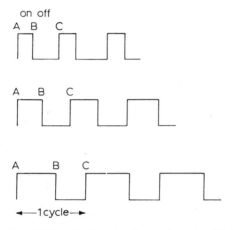

FIG. 7.9 Result of varying the on time of switching-mode circuit

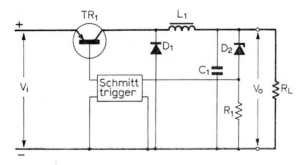

FIG. 7.10 Switching-mode circuit without separate pulse generator

When the load current is large the reverse obtains. When TR_1 is on, C_1 is only charged slowly and hence TR_1 remains on for a longer period, but when TR_1 is off, the voltage across C_1 falls quickly and hence TR_1 is off for a shorter period. In this way the ratio of time "on" to time "off" will vary, depending on the load current, but in all cases a constant mean voltage is maintained across C_1. Since there must be some variation of voltage across C_1, an additional smoothing circuit may be required. There are a number of variations of this general principle.

When thyristors are used the operation becomes more involved. A thyristor can be switched on by a suitable voltage applied to its gate. However, with a normal thyristor the current flow can only be stopped by some other means, such as reversal of the voltage on the anode. Thyristors which can be switched on and off by the gate are manufactured but are only available in small sizes and do not appear to have been used in this application. Normal thyristors will therefore be assumed.

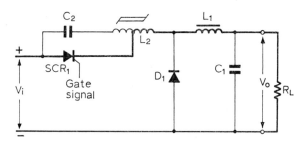

FIG. 7.11 Thyristor switching mode circuit

The upper part of the graphical symbol for L_2 indicates that the hysteresis loop is rectangular

One circuit used for switching off the thyristor, given in Fig. 7.11, is known as the *Morgan circuit*. In this circuit D_1, L_1 and C_1 from the normal switching circuit with the thryistor SCR_1 as the switching device. Capacitor C_2 and inductor L_2 have been added to switch off the thyristor. The core material of L_2 has a rectangular hysterisis loop, i.e. it has a high permeability until it becomes saturated, when the permeability becomes very low.

When SCR_1 is non-conducting the position is shown in Fig. 7.12 (*a*). The capacitor C_2 becomes charged in the direction shown, with a voltage equal to the difference between the input and output voltages, i.e. $V_i - V_o$. The thyristor is switched on by a pulse applied to the gate electrode, and when it is conducting a current i_L flows from the positive supply terminal

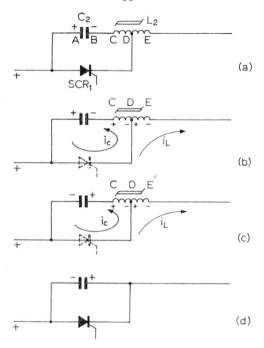

FIG. 7.12 Operation of thyristor switching circuit

through winding DE of the inductor L_1 and to the load. As the current rises a voltage is induced in winding DE with the polarity shown in at (*b*), i.e. such as to oppose the rise of current.

A voltage will also be induced in winding CD (by transformer action) with the polarity shown. This voltage and the voltage across the capacitor cause a current i_c to flow through the thyristor which first discharges the capacitor and then causes it to be charged in the opposite direction as in Fig. 7.12 (*c*). The current i_L flowing in winding DE causes the flux to increase until the core becomes saturated, and since there can now be no increase in flux the voltage induced in the windings is zero and the position is as shown at (*d*). The capacitor voltage now appears across the thyristor in the non-conducting direction, i.e. anode negative with respect to cathode. Hence the thyristor is switched off and remains off until another pulse is applied to the gate. During the time when the thyristor is off, C_2 discharges and recharges in the opposite direction back to the condition shown at (*a*).

The thyristor is therefore switched on by a pulse on its gate and switched off by the action of L_2, C_2. The "on" time is substantially constant, and control is therefore obtained by varying the "off" time, i.e. by varying the time between pulses fed to the gate. Thus to reduce the output voltage the time between pulses is increased, so decreasing the ratio of "on" to "off" time. Varying the time between pulses means, of course, that the frequency of operation is varied. There are a number of variations on this type of circuit, and circuits can be devised where two thyristors are used, one switching the circuit on and the other switching it off.

Switching-mode regulators have the advantages of high efficiency, say 90 per cent and more, and hence dissipate little power. This is of particular importance if the ratio of input voltage to output voltage is high, as dissipative types then become very inefficient. Switching-mode regulators have the disadvantage that the speed of correction is limited and generally less than that of dissipative types. Also there tends to be ripple on the output, and interference may be caused by the switching transients in the circuit.

TYPICAL FIGURES

Module with d.c. input: 30 V 5 A *supply*

Fraction stabilization ratio (S'), 2 000
Internal resistance, 0·002 Ω
Ripple, 15 mV r.m.s. (at 30 kHz) with 2 000/1 reduction of input ripple

References

1 GREENWOOD, I. A., HOLDAM, J. V., and MACRAE, D., *Electronic Instruments* (McGraw-Hill, 1948).
2 BENSON, F. A., "Initial drifts in running voltage of glow discharge regulator tubes," *J. Sci. Instrum.*, **27**, p. 71 (1950).
3 BENSON, F. A., "The characteristics of some miniature high-stability glow-discharge voltage-regulator tubes," *J. Sci. Instrum.*, **28**, p. 339 (1951).
4 BENSON, F. A., *Voltage Stabilized Supplies* (MacDonald, 1957).
5 BENSON, F. A., "Glow discharge tubes," *Radio Electron. Engng.*, **3**, pp. 23, 109, 193 (1962).
6 BENSON, F. A., and RIGG, B., "Temperature and pressure effects in glow-discharge reference tubes," *Proc. Instn Elect. Engrs.*, **110**, p. 29 (1963).
7 GOCKEL, H., "Über die Spannungskonstanz von Stabilovoltrohren bei Dauer-belastung", *Phys. Z.*, **38**, p. 65 (1937).
8 BENSON, F. A., CAIN, W. E., and CLUCAS, B. D., "Variations in the characteristics of some glow-discharge voltage-regulator tubes," *J. Sci. Instrum.*, **26**, p. 399 (1949).
9 TITTERTON, E. W. "Some characteristics of glow-discharge voltage-regulator tubes," *J. Sci. Instrum.*, **26**, p. 33 (1949).
10 PATCHETT, G. N., "Emitter follower as a constant voltage source," *Electron. Engng.*, **41**, p. 205 (Feb., 1969).
11 McPHERSON, J. W., "Regulator elements using transistors," *Electron. Engng.*, **36**, p. 162 (1964).
12 SHAFT, H. A., "Second breakdown—a comprehensive review," *Proc. Inst. Elect. Electron. Engrs.*, **55**, p. 1272 (1967).

142

List of Symbols

I_d r.m.s. output current of rectifier circuit
I_{dp} peak output current of rectifier circuit
I_o output current
i_d instantaneous output current of rectifier circuit
i_r instantaneous rectifier current
i_t instantaneous transformer secondary current
M regulator amplification
M_i regulator amplification of measuring unit across input
M_o regulator amplification of measuring unit across output
M_s regulator amplification of measuring unit in series with output
R_f regulation factor
R_f' fractional regulation factor
R_i internal resistance of stabilizer
R_L load resistance
R_o internal or output resistance
r_a valve a.c. resistance
S stabilization ratio
S' fractional stabilization ratio
V_D voltage across Zener diode
V_d r.m.s. output voltage of rectifier circuit
V_d' average output voltage of rectifier circuit
V_f' mean voltage across smoothing capacitor
V_i input voltage of stabilizer
V_{MU} voltage across measuring unit
V_o output voltage
V_{RU} voltage across regulating unit
V_{rp} peak voltage drop across rectifier in conducting direction
V_s r.m.s. supply voltage
V_t r.m.s. transformer secondary voltage (voltage of half the winding if it is centre tapped)
V_{tp} peak transformers secondary voltage (voltage of half the winding if it is centre tapped)
v_d instantaneous output voltage of rectifier circuit
v_{da} instantaneous alternating component of rectifier output voltage (across reservoir capacitor)

v_f instantaneous alternating component of voltage across smoothing capacitor

v_r instantaneous voltage across rectifier

v_s instantaneous supply voltage

v_t instantaneous transformer secondary voltage

β common-emitter current gain

μ valve amplification factor

Index